I0024361

George B. Rosher

**A Treatise on the Principles of Rating**

George B. Rosher

**A Treatise on the Principles of Rating**

ISBN/EAN: 9783337311933

Printed in Europe, USA, Canada, Australia, Japan

Cover: Foto ©Suzi / pixelio.de

More available books at **www.hansebooks.com**

# A TREATISE

ON THE

# PRINCIPLES OF RATING.

BY

GEORGE B. ROSHER., M.A.,

OF LINCOLN'S-INN AND OF THE SOUTH-EASTERN CIRCUIT, BARRISTER-AT-LAW.

LONDON:

W. MAXWELL & SON, 8, BELL YARD, TEMPLE BAR,
Law Booksellers and Publishers.

MEREDITH, RAY, & LITTLER, MANCHESTER;
HODGES, FIGGIS & CO., AND E. PONSONBY, DUBLIN;
CHARLES F. MAXWELL, MELBOURNE & SYDNEY.

1883.

# PREFACE.

THE principles of Rating, though founded on statute, are to a great extent the outcome of the judicial decisions of nearly three centuries. Those decisions have somewhat fluctuated from time to time, and though the author's object has been simply to present a statement of the law as it now exists, it has not always been possible to do so satisfactorily without to some extent tracing the course of its development. He has endeavoured to combine a lucid explanation of the principles of Rating, with such an arrangement of the subject as will facilitate reference to any required point.

The author desires to acknowledge his obligations to the first edition of Mr. E. J. Castle's work on the Law of Rating.

3, GARDEN COURT, TEMPLE.
*April,* 1883.

# TABLE OF CONTENTS.

———+———

———————————

. .

## PART I.—WHAT RATEABLE.

———————————

## PART II.—WHO RATEABLE.

# PART III.—HOW RATEABLE.

# TABLE OF CASES CITED.

43 Eliz. c. 2.

# PRINCIPLES OF RATING.

## INTRODUCTORY.

THE *raison d'être* of the law of Rating consists in the need of a methodical system of raising money for the relief of the poor. The foundation of existing law on the subject is the statute of the 43 Eliz. c. 2, which first outlined a system that has now been undergoing gradual development and modification, by judicial decisions and statutory enactments, for nearly three hundred years. *(The need of a law of rating,)*

Whether the enactment of such a statute as the 43 Eliz. c. 2 at that particular epoch was mainly due to the decay of the feudal system, under which the retainers and dependents of each feudal lord looked to him for support in times of need; or to the confiscation of monastery lands in the reign of Henry VIII., and the dissolution of the monastic societies which had previously been liberal dispensers of alms; or to some rapid increase in the numbers of the poor who required relief; it is not within the province of this work to inquire : suffice it to say, that, voluntary alms being found inadequate to the necessities and social conditions of the time, it was enacted in 1601, by the 43 Eliz. c. 2, as follows :— *(arose perhaps from the decay of the feudal system, or the dissolution of monasteries. Voluntary alms being inadequate, a compulsory system was required— The 43 Eliz. c. 2.)*

"Be it enacted by the Authority of this present Parliament, that the Churchwardens of every Parish, and four, *(The parish, the unit of area.)*

B

three or two substantial Householders there, as shall be thought meet, having respect to the Proportion and Greatness of the same Parish and Parishes, to be nominated yearly in Easter week, or within one month after Easter, under the Hand and Seal of two or more Justices of the Peace in the same County, whereof one to be of the Quorum, dwelling in or near the same Parish or Division **Overseers.** where the same Parish doth lie, shall be called Overseers of the Poor of the same Parish : And they, or the greater Part of them, shall take order from Time to Time, by, and with the Consent of two or more such Justices of Peace as is aforesaid, for setting to work the Children of all such whose Parents shall not by the said Churchwardens and Overseers, or the greater Part of them, be thought able to keep and maintain their Children : And also for setting to work all such Persons, married or unmarried, having no Means to maintain them, and use no ordinary and daily Trade of Life to get their Living by : And also to raise weekly or otherwise **Who and what is to be rated.** *(by Taxation of every Inhabitant, Parson, Vicar, and other, and of every Occupier of Lands, Houses, Tithes impropriate, Propriations of Tithes, Coal-mines, or Saleable Underwoods in the said Parish in such competent Sum* and Sums of Money as they shall think fit) a convenient Stock of Flax, Hemp, Wooll, Thread, Iron, and other necessary Ware and Stuff, to set the Poor on Work : And also competent sums of Money for and towards the necessary Relief of the Lame, Impotent, Old, Blind, and such other among them being Poor, and not able to work, and also for the putting out of such Children to be Apprentices, to be gathered out of the same Parish, according to the Ability of the same Parish, and to do and execute all other Things as well for the disposing of the said Stock, as otherwise concerning the Premisses, as to them shall seem convenient : " &c. &c.

**Object of the statute.**   The obvious intention of the statute was that all should bear a share of the burden of supporting the poor, in proportion to their means. In order to effect this, it constitutes in the first place a unit of area, namely the parish, and then provides for each parish, officers clothed with the duty of raising the sums required in that parish for the relief of the poor, by taxing, in due proportion, every parishioner, (*a*) in his capacity of inhabitant, and (*b*) in his capacity of occupier of lands, &c., that is, speaking generally, every holder of property, personal or real.

**How to be effected.**

**Subsequent modifications;**

In theory, the parish is still the unit of area, but in more modern times it has generally been found convenient and desirable in practice to group together a number of neighbouring parishes under the name of a Union, for the purposes of Poor-law administration.

**Unions.**

**Exemption of personalty.**

The dictates of convenience have also given rise to a much more important modification, namely the release of personal property, as such, from liability to rating. Owing to the difficulty of assessing personalty, the practice of doing so gradually fell into disuse in many parishes, and ultimately the exemption was legalised and made universal by statute in 1840.

**Parish the unit of area.**

In the first place then we find in the 43 Eliz. c. 2 that the parish is the unit of area; this we should naturally call the parochial principle, but that expression is commonly used in a more limited sense, to signify the rule of apportionment, of which the fact that the parish is the unit of area requires the adoption, where the subject of rating extends into more than one parish.

**Real but not personal property rateable.**

The second general rule is that real property is rateable, but personal property is not. This results from the 43 Eliz. c. 2, as modified by the 3 & 4 Vict. c. 89.

After ascertaining what description of property is rateable, the next thing to be decided is, who is to be rated in respect of it—the owner or the occupier—and on what principles is the assessment to be calculated. Before answering these

questions it will be well to read, in connection with the Act,
the clear and authoritative exposition of it in Sir Anthony
Earby's Case at Lincoln Assizes, in 1633,[1] which is thus
reported :—

*The exposition of the 43 Eliz. c. 2 in Sir Anthony Earby's case.*

"Upon complaint made to the Judges of Assize, by Sir
Anthony Earby, and others the inhabitants of the town of
Boston, upon an undue assessment made by the said town,
and overseers of the poor, and levied by them, the same
being, as was informed, undue and unequal, contrary to the
statute of 43 Eliz. c. 2 for provision to be made for the
poor, and contrary to former orders and directions given by
the Judges of Assize unto them, to make due and equal assessments.

Hereupon it was held, and so delivered for law, by
Haughton and Croke, Justices of Assize, that such assessments ought to be made according to the visible estate of the
inhabitants there, both real and personal, and that no inhabitant there is to be taxed by them to contribute to the
relief of the poor, in regard of any estate he hath elsewhere,
in any other town or place, but only in regard of the visible
estate he hath in the town where he doth dwell, and not for
any other land which he hath in any other place or town.

*The parish, the unit of area.*

And also by Hutton and Croke, Justices of Assize—This
hath been so resolved by all the Judges of England, upon a
reference made to them, and upon conference by them had
together, when they all did resolve that the assessment for
relief of the poor ought to be made in such manner as
before, according to their visible estates, real and personal,
which they had and enjoyed in the town or place where they
inhabited, and not having any regard to any other estate,
which they had in any other place or town.

*Property not to be rated*

*Nota.*—That Sir Anthony Earby complained also, that he,

---

[1] 2 Bulst. 354.

having divers tenants there which paid rent unto him, they *twice over—*
then did charge his tenants by their assessments, and did *the occupier rateable and*
charge himself also. *not the lessor.*

Upon this Mr. Leving, being counsel for the town of
Boston, did inform the Judges that they did tax Sir Anthony
Earby for his estate, he having the rents ; and that such an
assessment was made in the county of Leicester upon the
lessor, and that by the order and direction of the Judges of
Assize upon a complaint made unto them, and that they
were not to tax the tenants who paid the rents.

Hutton and Croke, Justices, made answer,—That they did
not remember any such case ; but they said, that by the
words and meaning of the statute of 43 Eliz. c. 2, they are
to assess the occupiers of the land, and not the lessor who
received the rents, the occupier of the land being by law
only to pay the assessment, unless it be specially provided
for as to this payment between him and his lessor, and so by
this to be discharged of this payment of such assessments.

The Judges did both of them agree to this, that by the
law, the occupiers of the land are only to be charged, and
this in regard of their possessions, and not the lessor, in
regard of the rents which he received; and so they declared,
that it hath been also thus resolved by all the Judges of
England : And so upon all this matter thus appearing to them.

The Judges here made their order according to the several *Rating to be*
resolutions, and this they did thus settle and order, for the *equal.*
better directions for the time to come : That they are to
make their taxations and assessments well and duly, and in
an equal manner, according to the visible estates, real and
personal, of such inhabitants within their town, and also to
tax and assess the occupiers of land within their town only,
and not the lessors, with a special charge to them given to
be careful in this for the future."

Here we find that the person liable to be rated is the occupier and not the lessor ; that all persons are to be rated in an equal manner, that is, on the same scale ; and that the same property is not to be rated twice over.

The principle that the parish is the unit of area is also emphasised by the judges in Sir Anthony Earby's case. They say that " no inhabitant there," i.e., in the parish under consideration, " is to be taxed . . . . to contribute to the relief of the poor in regard of any estate he hath elsewhere, in any other place or town."

**The cardinal principles of rating are found in the 43 Eliz. c. 2, and Sir Anthony Earby's case.**

Subject only to the modern exemption of personal property from rateability, the principles contained in the 43 Eliz. c. 2, as expounded in Sir Anthony Earby's case, are the cardinal principles of rating at the present day ; but the practical application of those principles,—especially in the case of some kinds of property which have but recently sprung into existence, such as railways, which extend through many parishes, and in that and other respects are of a different nature to anything that was contemplated in the early days of rating,—has given rise to questions of considerable intricacy.

In treating of the law of Rating in detail, it will be convenient to arrange it under three heads.

**I. What rateable.**

The first thing to be ascertained is,—What property is liable to rating? The intention of the 43 Eliz. c. 2 was, that everyone should contribute to the support of the poor in proportion to his means, whatever their nature ; but a very important exemption has arisen in the case of personal property, and there have also been some less important modifications of the statute of Elizabeth which will call for notice under this head.

**II. Who rateable.**

Having determined what is, and what is not, of a rateable nature, it becomes necessary in the second place to ascertain with respect to any property which is of a rateable nature,—Whether there is a person liable to be rated in respect of it? That will be found to depend on whether there is an 'occupier' within the statute.  Property may be in itself of a rateable nature, and yet there may be no person liable to be rated for it.  It will be seen that in order to create liability to rating, there must be a beneficial occupation, beneficial, *Beneficial occupn* that is, to some one, though not necessarily to the occupier. The occupier of a property, the outgoings of which exceed the receipts, is not rateable, because the occupation is not beneficial ; but if the receipts exceed the outgoings, then the occupier is rateable, although he may not derive any personal profit from it ; for instance, a corporation in occupation of docks, though bound to maintain them for the benefit of the public, and to apply all profits to public purposes, are nevertheless rateable in respect of those profits.  But where property is occupied by the Crown there is not an occupier within the statute, for the Crown not being named in the 43 Eliz. c. 2 is not bound by it ; and there are certain classes of occupiers who have been exempted from rating by subsequent statutes, on the ground of public expediency.

After having found a property of a rateable nature and a person liable to be rated in respect of it, the question arises, —How is the assessment to be calculated ?  The principle that rating is to be equal seems a simple one, but for the guidance of those whose duty it is to assess each of the various descriptions of rateable property in accordance with this principle, certain general rules have had to be settled, in the gradual development and definition of which, numerous questions, some of them of great nicety, have presented themselves for solution ; and the elucidation of these rules, and their bearing on different kinds of property, will occupy a comparatively large portion of this work.

III.
How rateable.

## PART I.

### WHAT RATEABLE.

## REAL BUT NOT PERSONAL PROPERTY RATEABLE.

THE 43 Eliz. c. 2 commands taxation (*a*) of every *inhabitant*, parson, vicar and other, and (*b*) of every *occupier* of lands, houses, tithes impropriate, propriations of tithes, coal mines or saleable underwoods in the parish.

Inhabitant rateable for personalty under 43 Eliz. c. 2. Two capacities are here designated in which a man should be liable to be rated. He might be rateable as an inhabitant of the parish, or as an occupier of property of one of the descriptions specified in the statute. In rating him as an occupier, the measure of his rateability is the annual value of the property occupied; in rating him as an inhabitant, the intention of the statute was that he should be rated according to his ability, as measured by his visible estate in the parish, *both real and personal*.

Earliest authorities. The earliest authorities unhesitatingly so interpret the statute. In the Resolutions of the Judges of Assize of 1633,[1] it is laid down, in answer to question 18, that the personal visible ability of the inhabitant may be taxed for the relief of the poor as well as the land ; and in Sir Anthony Earby's case,[2] in the same year, it was held that assessments ought to be made according to the visible estate of the inhabitants in the parish, both real and personal.

However, it appears that in some parishes personal property never was rated, and the custom of abstaining from rating it gradually became very general. This was probably owing to the difficulty and inconvenience experienced in attempting to assess it. The question of the rateability of personal property was from time to time brought before the Courts, and though they usually, at first at all events, declared without hesitation that personal property was legally rateable, there are not infrequent allusions in the reports to the fact that the custom of not rating it had become very general. In an exhaustive note to *R. v. Rodd,*[3] the condition of the question is stated to be, that the balance of authority was in favour of the rateability of personal property, but general practice and usage against it. In the latter part of the eighteenth century, however, the decisions, especially those in which Lord Mansfield was concerned, began to waver, and the Courts show a disposition to hesitate in affirming the rateability of personalty under the 43 Eliz. c. 2 apart from the usage hitherto prevailing in the parish in question.[4]

*Usage of some parishes not to rate personalty.*

*Decisions on the question.*

---

[1] Dalton's Country Justice, c. 73.
[2] 2 Bulst. 354.
[3] Cald. 149.
[4] The following cases bear on the rateability of personal property :—
*The case of the Parish of St. Leonard, Shoreditch* (1698), 2 Salk. 483 ; *R. v. Barking* (1706), 2 Lord Raymond, 1280; *R. v. Witney* (1760),
2 Wm. Bl. 709 ; *R. v. Canterbury* (1769), 4 Burr. 2290 ; *R. v. Ringwood* (1775), Cowp. 326 ; *R. v. Andover* (1777), Cowp. 550 ; *R. v. Hill* (1777), Cowp. 613 ; *R. v. Rodd* (1782), Cald. 147, 149 ; *Atkins v. Davis* (1783), Cald. 315 ; *R. v. Hogg* (1787), 1 T. R. 721 (per Buller, J.) ; *R. v. White* (1792), 4 T. R. 771 ; *R. v. Dursley*

Personality ignored by P. A. Act of 1836.

The Parochial Assessment Act of 1836 [1] seems to assume that the rateability of *personalty* was then obsolete, as after a preamble commencing, " Whereas it is desirable to establish one uniform mode of rating for the relief of the poor," the Act makes not the slightest allusion to the rating of personal property, or of an inhabitant as such.

R. v. Lumsdaine, 1839

Shortly after this Act, (in 1839,) a rate was appealed against [2] on the ground that it did not include stock-in-trade. It was argued that the Parochial Assessment Act,—which gave a form in which rates should be allowed for the future, which form did not allow for a rate on any property except real property and corporeal hereditaments,—was inconsistent with the continued rateability of personal property, and that it therefore abrogated pro tanto the 43 Eliz. c. 2. Lord Denman, C. J., in delivering judgment, admitted that it was not improbable that the legislature had intended to alter the law upon the subject of rating personal property, but said that if so, that intention could not be carried into effect but by an express enactment, nor could the Court regard the Parochial Assessment Act as having repealed the law as to the rateability of personalty by implication, and therefore the rate must be quashed.

Consequent action of Poor Law Commissioners.

Upon this decision the Poor Law Commissioners published a circular calling the attention of the parish authorities to the fact that every rate which omitted to include stock-in-trade would be liable to be quashed if appealed against. This rendered it necessary for the legislature to determine whether the 43 Eliz. c. 2 should be amended, or the general usage of not rating personalty replaced by a strict compliance with the Act as it stood. The legislature elected to amend the Act, being, no doubt, influenced by the inconvenience

---

(1794), 6 T. R. 53 ; *R.* v. *Darlington* (1795), 6 T. R. 468 ; *R.* v. *Ambleside* (1812), 16 East, 380.

[1] 6 & 7 Will. IV. c. 96.

[2] *R.* v. *Lumsdaine*, 8 L. J. M. C. 69 ; 10 A. & E. 157.

of carrying it out, as to which it may be mentioned that Difficulty of rating personalty. it had been laid down by Yates, J., in 1769, that "if personal property be rateable, it is not to be done at random, and to leave the party rated to get off as he can: but the officer making the rate must be able to support what he has done by evidence. <u>And no personal property can be rated but the clear liquidated surplus after paying all his debts.</u>" [1] It would be impossible therefore for the overseers to properly .rate personal property unless they were able to make, and actually did make, an examination of an inquisitorial description into the private affairs of individuals.

Accordingly in 1840 was passed the 3 & 4 Vict. c. 89, Exemption by 3 & 4 Vict. c. 89. which (temporarily) enacted that " it shall not be lawful for the overseers of any parish, township, or village, to tax any inhabitant thereof, as such inhabitant, in respect of his ability derived from the profits of stock-in-trade, or any other property, for or towards the relief of the poor.". The Act further provides that the liability of any parson or vicar or of any occupier of any of the descriptions of property specified in the 43 Eliz. c. 2 is not to be affected by it. <u>The effect therefore of the 3 & 4 Vict. c. 89</u> (which has been from time to time up to the present continued by Expiring Laws Continuance Acts), is to expunge the word " inhabitant " from the 43 Eliz. c. 2, and no one now (unless an incumbent is an exception in respect of his tithes) incurs liability to be rated in any other capacity than that of an occupier.

Subject then to certain exceptions, which will be specified General rule. hereafter, the general rule is that real property is rateable but that personal property is not.[2]

---

[1] Per Lord Kenyon, C. J. in *R.* v. *White*, 4 T. R. 771.

[2] The above statement must be taken only as an approximation to the truth. It is not easy to state the general rule in such a way as to be at

Whether it is consistent with the policy of the 43 Eliz. c. 2, which aimed at dividing the burden of supporting the poor fairly among all according to their respective means, that that burden should rest entirely on real to the exclusion of personal property, is a question into which it is not the province of this work to inquire; but it may be pointed out that the hardship, if such it is, is far greater at the present time, when there is much more personalty than realty in the country, than it was in those earlier times when the custom of not rating personalty was first adopted by the parishes, for in those days there was comparatively little personalty in existence, and it was not then an extravagant supposition that a man's real property was at all events a rough test of his ability to contribute.

## TITHES.

There are two classes of tithes,—those that are due to the incumbent; and those that are due to some other person.

The policy of the monastic orders[1] was to acquire advowsons whenever possible, and then to appropriate the benefices to the use of their own corporations. A portion of the tithes the appropriators bestowed by way of stipend on the priest

---

once concise, and in all respects accurate. For instance, real property is as a rule rateable, but one description of real property, namely, incorporeal hereditaments, are not rateable ; and again to this exception there is a further exception, for tithes and sporting rights, which are incorporeal hereditaments, are rateable,

and so on. Again, though the profits of trade are personal property, it will be found that Railway Companies are virtually, though not technically, rated on their trade profits. See pages 99 and 100, infra.

[1] Abridged from Stephen's Commentaries, Book IV., Part II., Chap. I., sec. 5.

whom they deputed to perform the spiritual duties. This portion was called the *vicarial tithes.* The remaining portion, which was reserved to the appropriators, was designated as *tithes appropriate,* or more shortly, *tithes propriate.* On the dissolution of monasteries the tithes appropriate vested in the Crown, and when they found their way, through the medium of Crown grants, into the hands of subjects who were laymen, they were called, by way of distinction, *tithes impropriate.*

Vicarial tithes.

Tithes appropriate.

Tithes impropriate.

An occupier of tithes appropriate or impropriate is clearly rateable under the 43 Eliz. c. 2, the words of which are, " by taxation of every inhabitant, parson, vicar or other, and of every occupier of lands, houses, tithes impropriate or propriations of tithes, coal mines or saleable underwoods in the said parish," &c.

Occupier of tithes severed from the incumbency rateable under 43 Eliz. c. 2.

But vicarial tithes not being mentioned in the occupation clause, it would seem to follow, on the principle of expressio unius exclusio est alterius, that an incumbent is not rateable for the vicarial tithes quâ 'occupier,' and that if rateable at all, it must be under the inhabitant clause. As to that it seems a plausible supposition that the parson and vicar were mentioned in the inhabitant clause merely to dispel any doubt as to their liability to be rated with the other inhabitants, which might arise from the words of Magna Charta, " quod ecclesia Anglicana libera sit." [1] But if the statute contemplated the rating of tithes vicarial, only as forming part of the ability of the incumbent in his capacity of 'inhabitant,' there would seem to be no logical justification for assessing him on the hard and fast rules as to the value of the occupation, by which those who are rateable as 'occupiers' are assessed. And if it be only in the capacity of 'inhabitant' that the incumbent is rateable in respect of his tithes, it

Tithes vicarial rateable if at all under the inhabitant clause.

---

[1] See *R.* v. *Hopkins,* 3 Keb. 255.

seems a hardship that he should be rated for them now that the rating of other inhabitants, as such, has been discontinued.[1]

*Rating of vicarial tithes in practice.*

However, vicarial tithes have always been regarded as rateable, and it seems to have been not uncommonly considered that it was in the capacity of 'occupier' that the parson was rateable for his tithes.

*Authorities on the rateability of vicarial tithes.*

The first record of the question of the rateability of a parson for his tithes having been raised is in the Resolutions of the Judges of Assizes, 1633,[2] where are to be found the following Question and Resolution in answer to it :—

*Resolutions of 1633.*

Qu. 33. " What proportion shall Parsonages or Tithes bear to the Taxation of the Poor of the Parish ? "

Resol. " The Parson or Vicar Presentative shall bear according to the reasonable Value of his Parsonage, having consideration to the just Deductions."

The form of the question implies that those who framed it regarded tithes in the hands of the parson as rateable, but opinions may differ as to the inference to be drawn from the answer.

*1709. R. v. Bartlett.*

In 1709 it was held, in *R.* v. *Bartlett*,[3] that, " A parson who lets his tithes to the parishioners may be taxed upon the poor-rate ; for the letting is but an agreement with the parishioners to retain the tithes, and the parson here has a modus for his tithes ; though it was objected that

---

[1] In Nolan's Poor Law, I. 126, the following reason is given for the rating of tithes vicarial :—"Tithes in the hands of the efficient incumbent, whether parson or vicar, are not expressly mentioned in the statute. But as it directs that the 'parson or vicar' shall be taxed, it must intend that it shall be for that property which constitutes the chief subject of their occupancy, tithes being deemed a tenement by our law."

[2] Dalton's Country Justice, edition of 1727, c. 73, p. 237.

[3] MS. Cases, Pasch. 7 Anne ; 16 Viner's Abridgement, 427.

the parishioners were occupiers, and so the parson not taxable."

The contention that the parson ought not to be rated, because in virtue of the letting the parishioners had become the occupiers, admits by implication that but for the letting the parson would have been the occupier of the tithes and as such rateable for them.

*R.* v. *Skingle*,[1] decided in 1718, is thus reported :—" The 43 Eliz. c. 2 charges lands, tenements, tithes, &c., to the poor's-rate.  By a private statute for erecting workhouses in Colchester, the poor are provided for in another manner, and the occupiers of lands and tenements are made chargeable : and after a rate an appeal is given to the sessions.  The defendant was parson and rated for his tithes, and appeals ; and because the word tithes was not in the Act of Parliament, which the sessions looked upon as an absolute repeal of the 43 Eliz. quoad Colchester, therefore they discharge him.  Et per curiam.  He ought not to be exempted but by express words, being liable before.  Here he is an occupier of a tenement, for tithes are a tenement.  Wherefore the order of sessions was quashed."

*1718.*
*R. v. Skingle.*

The fact that the 43 Eliz. c. 2 mentions not tithes generally, but only tithes propriate and propriations of tithes, i.e., the tithes that are not in the hands of the parson, is here entirely ignored.

In *R.* v. *Lambeth*,[2] which is somewhat similar to *R.* v. *Bartlett*, supra, it is said that the parson remains chargeable *as occupier* of the tithe although he receives a composition or a modus in lieu.

*1722.*
*R. v. Lambeth.*

In Dalton's Country Justice [3] it is laid down that " Every clergyman is to be rated for his glebe and tithes according to their yearly value, so long as they are in his own occupation,

*1727.*
*Dalton's Country Justice.*

---

[1] 1 Str. 100.
[2] 1 Str. 525.
[3] Edition of 1727, p. 254.

because the statute charges every occupier of tithes, &c., and the clergy are continued " (sic, but query—contained) "under those general words, unless particularly exempted."

This is another link in the chain of authorities which have established the rateability of an incumbent for his tithes, but we must take exception to the statement that the statute charges " every " occupier of tithes.

1789.
R. v. Carlyon.
In *R.* v. *Carlyon,*[1] decided in 1789, Lord Kenyon, C. J., says that "oblations and other offerings which constitute the rectorial *or vicarial* dues are rateable."

1814.
Nolan.
In Nolan's Poor Law,[2] ed. 1814, we find it stated that " not only parsonage houses and glebe lands are rateable in the hands of the occupier, but both rectorial and vicarial tithes have been always deemed so, whether due by common law or by custom."

1836.
6 & 7 Will. IV.
c. 71.
The Tithe Commutation Act of 1836 provides[3] that every rentcharge payable instead of tithes shall be subject to all parliamentary, parochial and county and other rates, charges and assessments, in like manner as the tithes commuted for such rentcharge have heretofore been subject.

1840.
3 & 4 Vict.
c. 89.
In the statute[4] which repealed, in 1840, the liability of inhabitants as such to be rated, there is an express exception "that nothing in this Act contained shall in anywise affect the liability of any parson or vicar," &c.

Summary.
Vicarial tithes are now rated like other subjects of rateable occupation, and the present practice is supported by the current of authority, and by statutory recognition.

A composition
in lieu of
tithe rateable
as the tithe
itself.
It was held before the Tithe Commutation Act, that a composition, modus, assessment or pension, payable to the parson in lieu of tithes was rateable in like manner as the tithes for which it may have been substituted, and by that

---

[1] 3 T. R. 385.
[2] Vol. I., p. 126.
[3] 6 & 7 Will. IV. c. 71, sec. 69.
[4] 3 & 4 Vict. c. 89.

Act it is expressly provided that every rentcharge payable instead of tithes shall be rateable in like manner as the tithes commuted for such rentcharge had been rateable.[1]

---

## COAL AND OTHER MINES.

### All mines are now rateable.

The 43 Eliz. c. 2 names as rateable, not mines in general, but, "coal mines" alone. Therefore in accordance with the well known rule of construction expressio unius exclusio est alterius, all mines other than coal mines were exempt from rateability under that statute.[2]

The only mines rateable under the 43 Eliz. c. 2 were coal mines,

But the exemption was removed by the Rating Act of 1874,[3] which provided[4] that mines of every kind not mentioned in the 43 Eliz. c. 2 should thenceforth be rateable.

but all mines have been rateable since the Rating Act of 1874.

The exemption of mines other than coal mines did not include quarries, so quarries have always been rateable under the head of 'lands.' Whether any particular excavation in the earth was a mine or a quarry was determined by the mode in which it was worked, not by the substance obtained from it. The term mine was therefore not limited to cases where metal was obtained, but there might be a clay mine or a stone mine.[5]

Quarries have always been rateable.

---

[1] *Lowndes* v. *Horne,* 2 Wm. Bl. 1252 ; *R.* v. *Toms,* Dougl. 401 ; *Rann* v. *Pickin,* Cald. 196 ; *R.* v. *Boldero,* 4 B. & C. 467 ; 6 Dow. & Ry. 557.

[2] *Morgan* v. *Crawshay,* L. R. 5 H. L. 304 ; 40 L. J. M. C. 202 ; *Lead Co.* v. *Richardson,* 3 Burr. 1341 ; 1 Wm. Bl. 389 ; *R.* v. *Cunningham,* 5 East 478 ; *R.* v. *Sedgley,* 9 L. J. (O. S.)

M. C. 61 ; 2 B. & Ad. 65 ; *R.* v. *Brettell,* 1 L. J. M. C. 46 ; 3 B. & Ad. 424.

[3] 37 & 38 Vict. c. 54.

[4] By sec. 3.

[5] *R.* v. *Dunsford,* 4 L. J. M. C. 59 ; 2 A. & E. 568 ; *R.* v. *Brettell,* 3 B. & Ad. 424 ; *R.* v. *Sedgley,* 1 L. J. M. C. 46 ; 2 B. & Ad. 65.

## SALEABLE UNDERWOODS, PLANTATIONS AND WOODS.

Saleable underwoods rateable under the 43 Eliz. c. 2.

The rule of construction which constituted the mention of coal mines in the 43 Eliz. c. 2 an exemption by implication of all other mines, gave to the mention in that statute of "saleable underwoods" the effect of an exemption of all wood-lands not used for the growth of saleable underwoods.

Plantations and woods rateable under the Rating Act of 1874.

The latter exemption was, like the former, abolished by the Rating Act of 1874, which extended the Poor-rate Acts to "land used for a plantation or a wood or for the growth of saleable underwood and not subject to any right of common."

"Land used for the growth of saleable underwoods" is a technically better expression than "saleable underwoods," the phrase of the 43 Eliz. c. 2, though practically they both amount to the same thing.

## RIGHTS OF SHOOTING, FISHING, ETC.

Sporting rights.

The rights of shooting, fishing, &c., are sometimes incident to the occupation of land, and sometimes are reserved to a person other than the occupier.

If incident to the occupation, rateable indirectly, as enhancing its value.

In the former case they are rateable indirectly, for to the extent to which they enhance the value of the occupation, the rateability of the occupier is increased in respect of them.

If severed from the occupation rateable under the Rating Act of 1874.

In the latter case, namely, when severed from the land, such a right was formerly not rateable, because it is merely an incorporeal hereditament,[1] but now by the Rating Act,

---

[1] *Hilton and Walkerfield v. Bowes,* L. R. 1 Q. B. 359; 35 L. J. M. C.    137; *Eyton v. Mold,* 6 Q. B. D. 13; 50 L. J. M. C. 39.

1874,[1] the Poor-rate Acts are extended to (inter alia) "rights of fowling, of shooting, of taking or killing game or rabbits, and of fishing, when severed from the occupation of the land."

## TURNPIKE AND OTHER TOLLS.

Tolls are not rateable per se,[2] for they do not come under any of the descriptions of property upon which rateability is imposed by the 43 Eliz. c. 2.

Although tolls are not directly rateable, quâ tolls, they are in some, but not all cases, rateable indirectly, viz. when they form part of the profits of the occupation of land. Bayley, J., says in R. v. Kingswinford,[3] "Tolls eo nomine are not rateable; but if the subject-matter out of which the tolls arise, be one mentioned in the statute of Elizabeth as the object of rate, then that may be rated by name, and the tolls which constitute its profits may be thus made to contribute to the relief of the poor." Turnpike tolls however are not rateable even indirectly.[4]

Whether in any particular instance tolls are indirectly rateable as enhancing the value of the occupation of a rateable subject, depends, not on any considerations peculiar to tolls themselves, but on general principles. It will however be convenient to refer shortly to the different kinds of tolls which have been dealt with in the numerous cases to be

*Tolls not rateable per se,*

*but in some cases are rateable indirectly as enhancing the value of the occupation.*

---

[1] 37 & 38 Vict. c. 54, s. 3, sub-s. 2.

[2] R. v. Nicholson, 12 East 330; R. v. Milton, 3 B. & Ald. 112; Williams v. Jones, 12 East 346; R. v. St. Mary, Leicester, 6 M. & S. 400; R. v. Macdonald, 12 East 324; R. v. Eyre, 12 East 416.

[3] 7 B. & C. 236; s.c. R. v. Dudley Canal Co., 6 L. J. (O. S.) M. C. 3.

[4] See page 26 infra.

found in the reports ; for instance, those of markets, harbours, lighthouses and ferries.

It will be found that the indirect rateability of any particular tolls (with the exception only of turnpike tolls which are exempted by statute[1]), depends on the following conditions :—

**Conditions under which tolls are indirectly rateable.**

—To make them rateable indirectly :—

1st. The person in receipt of the tolls must be an 'occupier' of land within the 43 Eliz. c. 2.

2nd. The tolls must be paid strictly for the use of the land.

**Illustrations.**

For example, if certain persons are authorised to improve, in order to make navigable, the channel of a river, and to take tolls, but their interest in the bed of the river amounts only to an easement, the tolls are not rateable, because the first condition is not satisfied.[2] Again if the proprietor of a lighthouse is entitled, by Crown grant, or by statute, to levy tolls on every ship passing by the lighthouse, those tolls are not rateable, for they are not, strictly speaking, the produce of the land ; they arise from a collateral obligation,[3] and as to ships which pass in the daytime, obviously are not paid for the use of the light. So with regard to the Drainage Rates levied by the Metropolitan Board of Works to defray the expenses of constructing and maintaining sewers, the liability to pay them attaches to property within the metropolis irrespective of any use the inhabitants or occupiers make of the sewers, and they therefore do not satisfy the second condition.[4]

The two tests above indicated will be further illustrated by the cases collected under the following heads, but it must be remembered that rateability depends on the facts of each case taken in conjunction with general principles, and not

---

[1] 3 Geo. IV. c. 126, s. 51, and 4 Geo. IV. c. 95, s. 31.

[2] *R.* v. *Mersey and Irwell Naviga- tion Co.*, 7 L. J. (O. S.) M. C. 70 ; 9 B. & C. 95.

[3] *R.* v. *Coke*, 5 L. J. (O. S.) M. C.

8 ; 5 B. & C. 797 ; *R.* v. *Fowke*, 5 B. & C. 814 n.

[4] *R.* v. *Metropolitan Board of Works*, L. R. 4 Q. B. 15 ; 38 L. J. M. C. 24.

on the particular description of tolls in question. Lighthouse tolls are as a rule not rateable, and canal tolls are as a
rule rateable, but this does not found a rule that tolls are
not rateable because they are lighthouse tolls, or that they
are rateable because they are canal tolls, it only shows that
the conditions under which lighthouse tolls are received are
as a rule similar inter se, and that the same may be said with
regard to canal tolls.

CANAL TOLLS.—A canal is land covered with water, and
under ordinary circumstances the bed of the canal is in the
occupation of the persons who receive the tolls, and the tolls
are paid for the use of the canal, and are therefore to be
taken into consideration as profits arising from, and therefore
enhancing the value of, the occupation of the land, and so
are indirectly rateable.[1] The tolls earned by a railway are
also clearly rateable in the same manner.

NAVIGATION DUES.—By navigation dues we usually mean
the tolls charged by those who have improved, in order to
render navigable, a naturally existing waterway, while the
expression canal tolls usually refers to tolls charged upon a
waterway that is entirely of artificial construction. The
only way in which the distinction bears upon the rateability
of the tolls, is that from the nature of a canal it is usually
the case that those in receipt of the tolls are ' occupiers,' for
the constructors of a canal have usually acquired the ownership of the land which forms its bed ; but the undertakers of
the improvement of a river are commonly persons who, while
leaving the ownership and occupation of the soil with those
to whom they originally belonged, have acquired merely the
rights necessary to enable them to improve and conduct the
navigation, and which may probably amount only to an

*Remarks on various kinds of tolls— Canal tolls.*

*Navigation dues.*

---

[1] *R.* v. *Milton*, 3 B. & Ald. 112 ; *R.*
v. *Palmer*, 1 B. & C. 546. Some old
cases in which canal tolls were held
rateable per se, were overruled by *R.*
v. *Nicholson*, 12 East 330.

easement. Where such is the case, the navigation dues are not indirectly rateable, because those who receive them are not 'occupiers' within the statute.[1] Where however the soil of the bed of the river is vested in the undertakers of the navigation, the navigation dues, or whatever they may be called, are indirectly rateable, for the undertakers are occupiers of land, and the dues are the profits of the land.[2]

**Lighthouse tolls or dues.** LIGHTHOUSE TOLLS OR DUES.—Since it has been decided that tolls *per se* are not rateable, attempts have been made, but without success, to rate lighthouse tolls in the hands of private persons[3] indirectly as profits of the occupation of the lighthouse. In *R.* v. *Coke*,[4] where the King had granted to Lord Lovell and his executors, &c., for sixty years, a certain lighthouse, with authority to maintain the lights, and also the right of charging tolls on passing ships, it was held that those tolls arose from a privilege and were not appurtenant to, so as to be profits of, the occupation. This case was shortly followed by *R.* v. *Fowke*,[5] where Bayley, J., in quashing a rate based as to amount on the value of the tolls of the lighthouse, said, "The tolls do not arise from the building, nor from anything of necessity connected with it."

**Dock and harbour dues.** DOCK AND HARBOUR DUES.—The indirect rateability of these, like other tolls, depends on whether both the above-

---

[1] *R.* v. *Mersey and Irwell Navigation Co.*, 7 L. J. (O. S.) M. C. 70 ; 9 B. & C. 95 ; *R.* v. *Thomas*, 9 B. & C. 139 ; *R.* v. *Aire and Calder Navigation Co.*, 8 L. J. (O. S.) M. C. 9 ; 9 B. & C. 820 ; *R.* v. *Aire and Calder Navigation Co.* (2nd case), 1 L. J. M. C. 24 ; 3 B. & Ad. 139 ; *R.* v. *Weaver Navigation Trustees*, 5 L. J. (O. S.) M. C. 102 ; 7 B. & C. 70 n. But such undertakers, though not rateable for the general navigation dues would be rateable for the dues of a lock or a sluice constructed on land purchased by them.

[2] *R.* v. *Portmore* (*Earl of*), 1 B. & C. 551 ; *Bath River Navigation Co.* v. *Willis*, 11 A. & E. 463 ; *R.* v. *London* (*Mayor of*), 4 T. R. 21. See also *R.* v. *Bristol Dock Co.*, 10 L. J. M. C. 105 ; 1 Q. B. 535 ; and *R.* v. *Kingston-upon-Hull Dock Co.*, 14 L. J. M. C. 114 ; 7 Q. B. 2.

[3] As to the tolls of lighthouses vested in the Trinity House, see page 34 infra.

[4] 5 L. J. (O. S.) M. C. 8 ; 5 B. & C. 797.

[5] 5 B. & C. 814 n.

mentioned conditions are satisfied. In *R.* v. *Kingston-upon-Hull Dock Co.*,[1] a company who were occupiers of the soil of certain docks were authorised by statute to take dues from all ships entering the port within which the docks were situated. As the port extended beyond the docks ships might become liable to these dues without coming on or using the property of the company, and it was held that the dues payable by such ships were not indirectly rateable, because not satisfying the condition of being paid strictly for the use of land. Lord Denman, C. J., said, "The toll given to the company, and which such ships are obliged to pay, is doubtless given *in respect of* the company having made those docks, but still it does not arise *from the use of* the docks, nor is it earned in them." But the dues received by the company from ships which did come into the docks themselves, and so used the property of the company, were held indirectly rateable as profits arising from the occupation.

In *Lewis* v. *Swansea*[2] the tolls in question, and which were held not rateable, were payable to the corporation of Swansea in respect of the landing and shipping of goods at the quays in Swansea harbour. The corporation were in fact occupiers of some of the quays, but they would have been equally entitled to the tolls without any such occupation, and therefore the tolls could not be regarded as profits of the occupation. In *R.* v. *Durham (Earl of)*[3] tolls payable by ships using a port were held indirectly rateable on the ground that, on the facts there existing, they were paid for the use of the soil and were not tolls in gross. These two cases were decided by the same principle, and the tolls were indirectly laid under contribution to the rates in the one case, while they escaped in the other, because the facts were in the opinion of the Court different.

*Lewis v. Swansea and R. v. Earl of Durham.*

---

[1] 14 L. J. M. C. 114; 7 Q. B. 2.
[2] 25 L. J. M. C. 33; 5 E. & B. 508.
[3] 28 L. J. M. C. 232; s. c. *Durham (Earl of)* v. *Bishopwearmouth*, 2 E. & E. 230.

Commis-
sioners of New
Shoreham
Harbour v.
Lancing.

Ferry tolls.

Market tolls
and stallage.

In *The Commissioners of New Shoreham Harbour* v. *Lancing*[1] tolls were payable by statute on ships entering the harbour. The Commissioners were not, under their Act, occupiers of the soil of the entrance but had merely an easement in it. So far, therefore, the first condition of rateability was not satisfied. It appeared however that they were in occupation of soil on which stood piers erected for the purpose of confining the channel; but as the tolls were not incident to, and would not have passed with, the occupation of these piers, the Court held that they did not come under contribution as being profits of the occupation.

FERRY TOLLS.—In *R.* v. *North and South Shields Ferry Co.*,[2] where the ferry in question was over the river Tyne, the Ferry Company were in occupation of the landing places on each side, but not of the land covered with water, over which the ferry boats passed. Lord Campbell, C. J., said that the use of the landing places was only a minor part of the consideration for the tolls, for they were earned mainly by the large capital employed in the boats, and by the transit of the boats, not over the land in the occupation of the company, but, over a tidal river: and further that this was not like the case of a canal company who occupy the whole line of land covered with water, over which the transit takes place, for here the landing places were the only land occupied by the company, and the tolls were not strictly for the use of them, and were not therefore indirectly rateable as profits of their occupation.

It appears from this, that if the Ferry Company had owned the bed of the river as well as the landing places, the tolls would have been indirectly rateable as profits of the occupation.

MARKET TOLLS AND STALLAGE.—Market tolls payable in

---

[1] L. R. 5 Q. B. 489 ; 39 L. J. M.      [2] 22 L. J. M. C. 9 ; 1 E. & B. 140.
C. 121.

obedience to the franchise of the market, whether a pre-scriptive or statutory one, on admission to the market or on goods sold in it, do not satisfy the conditions of indirect rate-ability, for they are tolls in gross and are not paid for the use of land; but stallage, i. e., the toll paid for the use of a stall in the market, is indirectly rateable, for it is paid for the occupation of the soil by a stall.[1]

The criterion is whether the toll is paid for the use of the soil, or merely in obedience to the franchise of the market. Where a toll paid on admittance to a market was not under the circumstances existing referable to a franchise, the Court held that it must consequently be paid for the user of the land, and therefore was to be indirectly rated among the profits of the occupation.[2]

In *London (Mayor of)* v. *Greenwich Union*, lairage dues, levied on the consignees of foreign cattle landed at Deptford Market, were held rateable indirectly, as being charges for the use and occupation of the soil. The case is not yet fully reported, but it appears[3] that the animals were allowed to remain in the lair a certain number of days, that no consignee had a right to the use of any particular lair, and that a charge was made, of so much per head of cattle landed, for wharfage, lairage, market dues, &c

## TURNPIKE TOLLS.

There is one description of tolls, which are in no circum-stances rateable, even indirectly, namely turnpike tolls, which

Turnpike tolls and toll-houses—statu-

---

[1] *R.* v. *Bell*, 5 M. & S. 221; *Roberts* v. *Aylesbury*, 22 L. J. M. C. 34; 17 J. P. 55; *London (Mayor of)* v. *St. Sepulchre*, L. R. 7 Q. B. 333 n.; 41 L. J. M. C. 109 n.; *R.* v. *Casswell*, L. R. 7 Q. B. 328; 41 L. J. M. C. 108; *Bedford (Duke of)* v. *St.*

*Paul, Covent Garden*, 51 L. J. M. C. 41; 45 L. T. N. S. 616.
[2] *Percy* v. *Ashford Union*, 34 L. T. N. S. 579.
[3] See 47 J. P. 148 and L. T. Mar. 3, 1883 p. 315.

tory exemp-
tion.

are exempt by statute, and the exemption extends to the toll-houses themselves.

3 Geo. IV. c. 126, s. 51.

It is provided by the 51st section of the Turnpike Act of 1822,[1] that "no tolls to be taken at any gate erected, or to be erected by the trustees or commissioners of any turnpike road, *nor toll-house* erected, or to be erected, for the purpose of collecting the same, nor any person in respect of such tolls *or toll-house,* shall be rated or assessed of any poor's rates, or any other public or parochial levy whatsoever." The provisions of this section were slightly extended by the 31st

4 Geo. IV. c. 95, s. 31.

section of the Turnpike Act of the following year, the 4 Geo. IV. c. 95, which provided that "no tolls or penalties for overweight to be taken at any house or weighing machine erected, or to be erected, or adjoining to any turnpike road, nor any person whatsoever in respect of such tolls or penalties, *or any house or building as aforesaid,* shall be rated or assessed towards the payment of any poor's rates, or any other public or parochial rate or levy whatsoever."

As to what roads are turnpikes within these Acts, see *R.* v. *Great Dover Street Road Trustees.*[2]

## EXEMPTION OF CHURCHES AND OTHER PLACES OF WORSHIP AND DISCRETIONARY EXEMPTION OF SUNDAY AND RAGGED SCHOOLS.

3 & 4 Will. IV. c. 30.

Churches and other places of public religious worship are exempted by the 3 & 4 Will. IV. c. 30, which enacted "that from and after the 1st day of October, 1833, no person shall be rated or shall be liable to be rated to or to pay any church or poor rates or cesses, for or in respect of any

---

[1] 3 Geo. IV. c. 126.          [2] 6 L. J. M. C. 25; 5 A. & E. 692.

churches, district churches, chapels, meeting-houses, or premises or such part thereof as shall be exclusively appropriated to public religious worship, and which (other than churches, district churches, and episcopal chapels of the Established Church) shall be duly certified for the performance of such religious worship according to the provision of any Act or Acts now in force: Provided always, that no person or persons shall be hereby exempted from any such rates or cesses for or in respect of any parts of such churches, district churches, chapels, meeting-houses, or other premises which are not so exclusively appropriated, and from which parts not so exclusively appropriated such person or persons shall receive any rent or rents, or shall derive profit or advantage. *Premises exclusively appropriated to religious worship exempt.*

Provided always, that no person or persons shall be liable to any such rates or cesses because the said churches, district churches, chapels, meeting-houses, or other premises, or any vestry-rooms belonging thereto, or any part thereof, may be used for Sunday or Infant Schools, or for the charitable education of the poor." *The exemption not lost by their being used for Sunday, infant, or charity schools.*

## SUNDAY AND RAGGED SCHOOLS.

The rating authorities may if they choose, but are not obliged to, exempt Sunday and ragged schools. *Discretionary exemption of Sunday and ragged schools by 32 & 33 Vict. c. 40.*

The 32 & 33 Vict. c. 40 enacts that " from and after the 30th day of September, 1869, every authority having power to impose or levy any rate upon the occupier of any building, or part of a building, used exclusively as a Sunday school or ragged school, *may* exempt such building, or part of a building, from any rate for any purpose whatever which such authority has power to impose or levy."

The Act goes on to provide that nothing in it contained " shall prejudice the right of exemption from rating of Sunday or infant schools, or for the charitable education of the poor in any churches, district churches, chapels, meeting-houses, or other premises, or any vestry rooms belonging thereto, or any part thereof," given by the 3 & 4 Will. IV. c. 30 (see supra, page 26), and it defines a " Sunday school," as, " any school used for giving religious education gratuitously to children and young persons on Sundays, and on week days for the holding of classes and meetings in furtherance of the same object, and without pecuniary profit being derived therefrom;" and a " Ragged school," as, " any school used for the gratuitous education of children and young persons of the poorest classes, and for the holding of classes and meetings in furtherance of the same object, and without any pecuniary benefit being derived therefrom except to the teacher or teachers employed."

*Definition of Sunday school.*

*Definition of Ragged school.*

*The exemption discretionary.*

It was contended in *Bell* v. *Crane*[1] that "may exempt" should be construed as "must exempt," having regard to the preamble of the Act, which is as follows :—"Whereas for many years and until lately,[2] buildings used as Sunday and ragged schools for gratuitous education, enjoyed an exemption from poor and other rates, and it is expedient that they should be exempted from such liability—Be it therefore enacted," &c. But the Court held that the phrase "may exempt" was intended to give, and does give, a discretion.

## EXEMPTION OF PROPERTY OCCUPIED BY LITERARY, SCIENTIFIC AND ARTISTIC SOCIETIES.

*Literary, scientific, and artistic societies.*

The 6 & 7 Vict. c. 36 enacted (sec. 1) that "from and after the 1st day of October, 1843, no person or persons shall be assessed or rated, or liable to be assessed or rated, or liable to pay, to any county, borough, parochial, or other local rates or

---

[1] L. R. 8 Q. B. 481 ; 42 L. J. M. C. 122.

[2] i. e. until the Mersey Dock cases, about four years previous to this Act.

cesses in respect of any land, houses, or buildings, or parts
of houses or buildings, belonging to *any society instituted*
*for purposes of science, literature, or the fine arts exclusively,*
either as tenant or owner, and occupied by it for the transaction of its business, and for carrying into effect its purposes,
provided that such society shall be *supported wholly or in*
*part by annual voluntary contributions,* and *shall not, and*
*by its laws may not, make any dividend, gift, division or*
*bonus in money into or between any of its members,* and provided also that such society shall obtain the certificate of the
barrister-at-law, or Lord Advocate, as hereinafter mentioned."

Subsequent sections provide that any society claiming to
be exempted under this Act is to submit its rules, in England
to the barrister for the time being appointed to certify the
rules of friendly societies, and in Scotland to the Lord Advocate, and must obtain from him, as a condition precedent to
exemption, a certificate that the society is entitled to the
benefit of the Act,[1] but that if such certificate be refused, the
society may appeal to the Quarter Sessions.[2]

*Procedure for obtaining exemption.*

The certificate however if granted is not conclusive proof
of a right to exemption. In *R.* v. *Phillips,*[3] the Court of
Queen's Bench, holding that the facts did not sustain the
certificate which had been granted to a society called the
Birmingham News Room, granted a mandamus commanding
the justices to issue their distress warrant for the recovery of
the sum at which the society's premises had been rated.

*Certificate not conclusive.*

## *"Any society instituted for purposes of science, literature or the fine arts exclusively."*

It will be convenient first to consider what societies have
been held to come within these words, secondly to point out

---

[1] Sections 2—5.
[2] Section 6.
[3] 17 L. J. M. C. 83 ; 8 Q. B. 745.

that the promotion of science, literature or the fine arts must be the primary and not merely a secondary object of the society, and thirdly to show the force of the word " exclusively."

What societies within the Act.

Examples.

1. **What societies do and what do not fall within these words.** The following Societies have been held not within the Act :—The Religious Tract Society,[1] which it was argued came under the head of literary societies, but this contention was unsuccessful, for its purpose is the advancement, not of literature in general, but of religion ; the Baptist Missionary Society ;[2] a Society for the promotion of education in general and the elucidation of the art of teaching ;[3] the United Service Institution ;[4] the Zoological Society of London ;[5] and

Societies not within the Act.

the Russell Institution in Bloomsbury.[6] But the following societies have been held within the Act :—A Society for the purpose of creating and maintaining a library for the use of members and subscribers ;[7] a Society the main purpose of which is to provide lectures on literature and science and exhibitions of paintings ;[8] the Linnæan Society for the cultivation of Natural History ;[9] and the Botanic Gardens of the University of Oxford.[10]

Primary and not merely

2. **The promotion of science, literature or the fine arts**

[1] *R.* v. *Jones,* 15 L. J. M. C. 29 ; 8 Q. B. 719.

[2] *R.* v. *Baptist Missionary Society,* 18 L. J. M. C. 194 ; 10 Q. B. 884.

[3] *R.* v. *Pocock,* 15 L. J. M. C. 132 ; 8 Q. B. 729.

[4] *R.* v. *Cockburn and others,* 16 Q. B. 480 ; s. c. *R.* v. *St. Martin's-in-the-Fields,* 21 L. J. M. C. 53.

[5] *Marylebone* v. *Zoological Society of London,* 23 L. J. M. C. 139 ; 3 E. & B. 807.

[6] *Russell Institution* v. *St. Giles-in-the-Fields, and St. George's, Bloomsbury,* 23 L. J. M. C. 65 ; 3 E. & B. 416.

[7] *Birmingham (Churchwardens of)* v. *Shaw,* 10 Q. B. 868 ; s.c. *Re Birmingham New Library,* 18 L. J. M. C. 89 ; *Clarendon (Earl of)* v. *St. James', Westminster,* 20 L. J. M. C. 213 ; 10 C. B. 806 ; *Liverpool Library* v. *Liverpool (Mayor of),* 29 L. J. M. C. 221 ; 5 H. & N. 526.

[8] *R.* v. *Manchester,* 20 L. J. M. C. 113 ; 16 Q. B. 449.

[9] *Linnæan Society* v. *St. Anne's, Westminster,* 23 L. J. M. C. 148 ; 3 E. & B. 793.

[10] *Re Oxford Poor Rate,* 27 L. J. M. C. 33 ; 8 E. & B. 184.

must be the primary, and not merely a secondary object of the society. The premises of a society called the Manchester Concert Hall, were held rateable on the ground that the promotion of the fine arts was not the primary, but only an incidental object of the society, the primary object being the gratification of its members ;[1] the Institution of Civil Engineers was held rateable on the ground that its primary object was the advancement of scientific knowledge, not in general, but among its own members for the purpose of the pursuit of their profession as civil engineers ;[2] a literary and newsroom society was held rateable on the ground that it was established primarily for the improvement and convenience of its own members, and not for the promotion of the general literature of the country ;[3] and the Zoological Society was held rateable on the ground that its primary object was the amusement of its subscribers.[4]

*secondary object of the society.*

The object of a society is to be judged not so much by its written laws and constitution as by what it actually does in practice.[5]

*Actual facts a better test of the object than written laws.*

3. **"Exclusively."** A society loses its title to exemption if it lets portions of its premises to other societies,[6] even though they pay only such sums as are equivalent to the cost of firing, lighting and cleaning, so that no profit is made,[7] or though the rent received is added to the funds and spent on the purposes of the society.[8] But where some of the

*Exclusively— Use of rooms by others takes away the exemption,*

*except where they occupy*

---

[1] *R.* v. *Brandt,* 20 L. J. M. C. 119 ; 16 Q. B. 462.

[2] *R.* v. *Institution of Civil Engineers,* 5 Q. B. D. 48 ; 49 L. J. M. C. 34.

[3] *R.* v. *Gaskill,* 21 L. J. M. C. 29 ; 16 Q. B. 472.

[4] *Marylebone* v. *Zoological Society of London,* 23 L. J. M. C. 139 ; 3 E. & B. 807.

[5] *Purchas* v. *Parish of the Holy Sepulchre, Cambridge,* 24 L. J. M. C.

9 ; 4 E. & B. 156, per Wightman, J. ; *Scott* v. *St. Martin's-in-the-Fields, Westminster,* 25 L. J. M. C. 42 ; 5 E. & B. 558 ; *Purvis* v. *Traill,* 18 L. J. M. C. 57 ; 3 Ex. 344.

[6] *Clarendon (Earl of)* v. *St. James', Westminster,* 20 L. J. M. C. 213 ; 10 C. B. 806.

[7] *R.* v. *Baptist Missionary Society,* 18 L. J. M. C. 194 ; 10 Q. B. 884.

[8] *Purvis* v. *Traill,* 18 L. J. M. C. 57 ; 3 Ex. 344.

**as servants of the society,** | rooms were occupied by a clerk, librarian, and porter, whose residence was subsidiary and necessary to the purposes of the society, such occupation did not deprive the society of exemption : neither did the fact that a portion of the premises was let off, which was capable of being, and was, separately

**or where there can be a separate rating.** | rated in the hands of the tenant.[1] So in the case of the Botanic Garden at Oxford, the residences of the Professor of Botany, the gardener, and the porter were held rateable separately, while not affecting the exemption of the garden itself.[2]

**Voluntary contributions.**

*"Supported, wholly or in part, by annual voluntary contributions."*

**To be voluntary a contribution need not be gratuitous,** | In *Birmingham (Churchwardens of)* v. *Shaw,*[3] it was held that in order to entitle subscriptions to be regarded as voluntary, it is not necessary that they should produce no kind of return to the contributors. It was argued that "voluntary" means "gratuitous," and that the subscriptions must not entitle the subscriber himself to any personal benefit, but Lord Denman, C. J., said, "Upon consideration we think that annual contributions will satisfy the condition required, if they commence of the party's own choice, are so continued, and may be withdrawn at pleasure, that is without subjecting the party to any legal liability or forfeiture beyond that of foregoing a participation in the pleasure or profit, scientific, literary or artistic, in respect of which they

**but only not legally compulsory.** | have been made. If the contributor was free to commence his contribution, and incurs no legal obligation to continue it when he has once commenced, and upon ceasing to contribute will lose no more than the privileges of membership, in respect of which he became a contributor, it seems to us that

---

[1] *Linnæan Society* v. *St. Anne's, Westminster,* 23 L. J. M. C. 148 ; 3 E. & B. 793.

[2] *Re Oxford Poor Rate,* 27 L. J. M.

C. 33 ; 8 E. & B. 184.

[3] 10 Q. B. 868 ; s.c. *Re Birmingham New Library,* 18 L. J. M. C. 89.

he must be considered a voluntary contributor, unless we add something to the idea of voluntariness which in ordinary language it does not import. And that is what, in fact, is done by those who contend that it must be also gratuitous and bring no return of any kind to the contributor; against the addition of which particular qualification there is the further reason that the statute itself, in the clause next to be considered,[1] provides for this expressly, and so seems to exclude the notion of its being previously implied."

In *The Linnæan Society* v. *St. Anne's, Westminster,*[2] Lord Campbell, C. J., said, "Although contributions are made by the fellows of the society, and they are under an engagement to pay so long as they are fellows, still they are voluntary, because it was under a voluntary engagement originally entered into that the obligation was incurred, and they voluntarily remain members of the society."

The two last mentioned cases were followed in *R.* v. *Bradford*;[3] and in *The Liverpool Library* v. *Liverpool (Mayor of)*,[4] it was held that an institution called the Liverpool Library was not taken out of the exemption by the fact that a subscription of a guinea a year entitled the subscriber to a transferable share in the institution, which share had a market value.

*A share in the institution.*

" *Shall not, and by its laws may not, make any dividend, gift, division or bonus in money unto or between any of its members.*"

It is not sufficient, to qualify a society for exemption, that no dividend, &c., has in fact ever been made or contemplated, but it must be expressly provided by the laws of the society

*There must be no dividend,*

*and no possibility of a dividend.*

---

[1] i.e., the clause which provides that no member shall receive any dividend, &c.

[2] 23 L. J. M. C. 148 ; 3 E. & B. 793.

[3] 28 L. J. M. C. 73 ; 1 E. & E. 88.

[4] 29 L. J. M. C. 221 ; 5 H. & N. 526.

that no dividend, &c., shall be made.[1]  But the profit which a subscriber might make by transferring his share in the society is not within the words " dividend, gift, division, or bonus in money."[2]

**Division of proceeds on dissolution of the society.**

Neither does a society while it exists lose its right to exemption merely because it might at some future time be dissolved and its property then sold and the proceeds divided amongst its members.[3]

## EXEMPTION OF STOREHOUSES OF VOLUNTEER CORPS.

**Volunteer storehouses exempt from rates.**

The 26 & 27 Vict. c. 65 enacts by section 26 as follows :—
" The commanding officer of a volunteer corps or administrative regiment, receiving any arms, ammunition, or other stores supplied at the public expense, or by subscription, shall subject to the approval of the lieutenant of the county, to which the corps belongs, or in which the head-quarters of the administrative regiment are situate (as the case may be), appoint a proper storehouse for the depositing and safe keeping of such arms, ammunition or stores.  Every such storehouse shall be free from all county parochial or other local rates and assessments."

## EXEMPTION OF LIGHTHOUSES, ETC.

**Lighthouses, buoys, beacons, &c.,**

The Merchant Shipping Act, 1854 (17 & 18 Vict. c. 104), enacts, by section 430, that all lighthouses, buoys, beacons,

---

[1] *R.* v. *Jones* (the Religious Tract Society case), 15 L. J. M. C. 129 ; 8 Q. B. 719.

[2] *Birmingham* (*Churchwardens of*) v. *Shaw*, 10 Q. B. 868 ; s.c. *Re*

*Birmingham New Library*, 18 L. J. M. C. 89.

[3] *Ib.* and *R.* v. *Manchester*, 20 L. J. M. C. 113 ; 16 Q. B. 449.

and light-dues, and all other rates, fees, or payments, accru-  exempt from rates.
ing to, or forming part of, the Mercantile Marine Fund, and
all premises or property belonging to, or occupied by, the
Board of Trade or any of the general lighthouse authorities
constituted by the Act, which are used or applied for the
purposes of any of the services for which such dues, rates,
fees and payments are received, and all instruments or
writings used by, or under the direction of, any of the
general lighthouse authorities or the Board of Trade, in
carrying on the services of lighthouses, buoys or beacons,
shall be exempted from all public, parochial and local taxes,
duties, and rates of every kind.

---

There is also what is not quite accurately called the  Property in Crown occu-
exemption of Crown property. This will be discussed when  pation not
we come to the consideration of under what circumstances  rateable,
there is a rateable occupier, of property which is in itself of a
rateable nature, for property is exempted, not because it is
Crown property in the sense of belonging to the Crown, but
because when it is occupied by the Crown there is not an  because the Crown is not
'occupier' within the 43 Eliz. c. 2, for that statute only  an 'occu-
applies to subjects, the Crown not being bound by it because  pier' within the statute.
not named in it.

Perhaps some of the exemptions already dealt with, that of
property occupied by literary, scientific or artistic societies
for instance, should in strictness be placed under the head of
exempted occupiers (in Part II.) rather than treated as
exempted descriptions of property (in Part I.), but it appears
convenient to place all the statutory exemptions together.

## ELEMENTS OF RATEABLE OCCUPATION.

HAVING found a property which is in itself of a rateable nature, the next thing to be ascertained is whether there is a person who can be rated in respect of it; that is to say, Is there an occupier?

**Poor-rate a personal tax on the occupier.**

The Poor-rate is a *personal* tax. It is a charge in respect of land but it is not a charge on the land, payable out of it, like the Land Tax.[1] The person to be rated in respect of land is by the 43 Eliz. c. 2 the *occupier*, but unless a person can be found who is an occupier within the statute there is no one from whom the rate can be collected,[2] as the charge does not attach directly to the land itself. Therefore, the question of what constitutes occupation within the statute is an

---

[1] *Case* v. *Stephens*, Fitzg. 297; *Theed* v. *Starkey*, 8 Mod. 314.

[2] *Holford* v. *Copeland*, 3 Bos. & Pul. 129, at 141; *R.* v. *London (Mayor of)*, 4 T. R. 21, at 26; *R.* v. *York (Mayor)*, 6 L. J. M. C. 121, at 125; 6 A. & E. 419, at 432; *Smith* v. *Birmingham (Guardians of)*, 26 L. J. M. C. 105, at 109; 7 E. & B. 483, at 489; *Rowls* v. *Gells*, Cowp. 451; *R.* v. *St. Luke's Hospital*, 2 Burr. 1053, at 1066; *R.* v. *Commissioners of Salter's Load Sluice*, 4 T. R. 730.

important one.  In a written judgment delivered in 1877,[1] What consti-<br>tutes occupa-<br>tion. Lush, J., says "It is not easy to give an accurate and exhaustive definition of the word ' occupier.'  Occupation includes pos- Possession. session as its primary element but it also includes something more.  Legal possession does not of itself constitute an occupation.  The owner of a vacant house is in possession, and may maintain trespass against anyone who invades it, but as long as he leaves it vacant he is not rateable for it as an occupier.  If, however, he furnishes it and keeps it ready for Actual user. habitation whenever he pleases to go to it, he is an occupier, though he may not reside in it one day in a year.  On the Title imma-<br>terial. other hand, a person, who, without having any title, takes actual possession of a house or a piece of land, whether by leave of the owner or against his will, is the occupier of it. Another element, however, besides actual possession of the land, is necessary to constitute the kind of occupation which the Act contemplates, and that is permanence.  An itinerant Permanence. showman who erects a temporary structure for his performances, may be in exclusive possession, and may, with strict grammatical propriety, be said to occupy the ground on which his structure is placed, but it is clear that he is not such an occupier as the statute intends.  As the poor rate is not made day by day or week by week, but for months in advance, it would be absurd to hold that a person, who comes into a parish with the intention to remain there a few days or a week only, incurs a liability to maintain the poor for the next six months.  Thus a transient temporary holding of land is not enough to make the holding rateable.  It must be an occupation which has in it the character of permanence ; a holding as a settler not as a wayfarer."

Four points are here indicated under which the cases on occupation may be grouped.  There must be possession, there must be actual user, and the occupation must be of a

---

[1] *R.* v. *St. Pancras,* 2 Q. B. D. 581 ; 46 L. J. M. C. 243.

permanent character, but title is immaterial if possession
exists. There is also another requisite, namely, the occupation must be beneficial in order to be rateable.

Occupation
must be
beneficial.

Before examining in detail the elements of the rateable
occupation of land, it may be pointed out that land includes
not only the face of the earth but every thing under it or
over it,[1] so that there may be a rateable occupation below
the surface by the pipes of a water company, buried in the
earth,[2] and above the surface by the wires of a telegraph
company, suspended in the air,[3] as well as an occupation of
the surface itself by a third party.

There may be
a rateable
occupation
above or below
as well as on
the surface.

## POSSESSION.

The primary element of occupation is possession, and
without possession there can be no occupation.

A person who has only an easement, or license, or anything short of possession of the soil is not rateable. This
is recognised in Sir Anthony Earby's case,[4] in which it is
specified that assessments are to be made according to
" *visible* estates." The limitation of rateability to " visible
estates " excludes incorporeal hereditaments,[5] such as easements and licenses in the nature of easements, and it proceeds apparently on the ground that there can be no occupier
of property which is of such a nature that possession of it
cannot be delivered, possession being essential to occupation. This view seems to be adopted by Bayley, J. in *R.* v.
*Churchill,*[6] where he says, " Land lies in livery, but a right
of common in grant. Does that for which it is attempted to
rate the burgesses of Nottingham lie in grant or in livery ?

There must
be possession
of the soil.

Easement or
license insuffi-
cient.

No livery of
seisin of
incorporeal
hereditaments.

---

[1] Burn's Justice, 29th ed., vol. iv.
190 (citing Blackstone) ; quoted by
Martin B. in *Electric Telegraph Co.* v.
*Salford,* 24 L. J. M. C. 146 ; 11 Ex. 181.

[2] *R.* v. *Bath (Corporation of)*, 14
East 609.

[3] *Electric Telegraph Co.* v. *Salford,*
24 L. T. M. C. 146 ; 11 Ex. 181.

[4] 2 Bulst. 354.

[5] Tithes and sporting rights are exceptions.

[6] 4 B. & C. 750 ; 6 Dow. & Ry. 635.

Each has a right to turn three head of cattle upon certain fields during a certain portion of the year. It is claimed by them as burgesses and as occupiers of ancient houses. Could they be enfeoffed of such a privilege ? If not it is plain that they have no right to the soil, but merely an incorporeal hereditament, a right of common by prescription, which is not rateable," and in *Kempe* v. *Spence*,[1] De Grey, C. J., lays down that a right of common being an incorporeal hereditament is not a subject of occupation.

There is no doubt that an easement is not rateable,[2] but it is sometimes difficult to say whether a given use of land amounts to occupation or only to an easement, in other words, whether the person it is sought to rate, is or is not in possession of the soil. Possession, moreover, to be rateable must be exclusive, i.e., while the occupation exists there must be neither any control or power of control in the grantor, nor any similar rights over the same subject matter in other grantees. As it is expressed in Nolan's Poor Law,[3] —as between himself and the grantor, " it is necessary not only that the person should have possession, but that he should have such a control and dominion over the subject, as implies freedom from any paramount occupation, or direct interference by a superior with his domestic arrangements and internal management ; such as a farmer enjoys over his farm, and the master of a family over his house." As against other grantees, possession to be exclusive must be unattended by any similar and simultaneous rights in any other person in respect of the same subject matter, and where any such have been granted, or can be granted, to other persons, it is not a case of exclusive possession.[4]

*[side notes: Possession must be exclusive, both of the grantor, and of all other persons.]*

---

[1] 2 Wm. Bl. 1244.
[2] *R.* v. *Alnwick*, 8 L. T. M. C. 50; 9 A. & E. 444; *R.* v. *Mersey and Irwell Navigation Co.*, 7 L. T. (O. S.) M. C. 70; 9 B. & C. 95 (per Parke, J.);

*Hilton and Walkerfield* v. *Bowes*, L. R. 1 Q. B. 359 ; 35 L. J. M. C. 137.
[3] Vol. I., 152, 153.
[4] *R.* v. *Tewkesbury*, 13 East 155.

There must be possession of the soil, as distinguished from easement or license, and possession that is exclusive both of dominant control by superiors and simultaneous rights in equals, before any one can be rateable as an occupier.  If he can show that one of these conditions is not satisfied in his case he is not rateable.  A person may have the exclusive enjoyment of the occupation, the sole use of moorings for instance,[1] and yet not be an occupier, because falling short of possession of the soil ; while on the other hand a person may be in possession in the ordinary sense of the word, as for instance a lodger, and yet not be an occupier, because subject to a paramount occupation by the landlord, or he may escape rateability simply because the owner of the property, of which he is in fact the only person in enjoyment, has the right of granting similar privileges to others.[2]

*There may be exclusive enjoyment without rateable occupation.*

Blackburn, J., said, in *Watkins* v. *Milton-next-Gravesend*,[3] " There may be a grant of many easements which are conveyed solely to one person and yet do not confer any occupation, such as a wayleave to carry coals from a colliery to the sea shore ; an important right confined to that colliery alone ; that does not make the person who has the sole use of a private way over the land rateable ; or in the more familiar case of a lodger who has the sole right to the use of certain rooms in a house, he is not made by that means rateable if the agreement is that the tenant of the house shall retain the possession, as in the general case of a lodging he does, for the purpose of looking after the management of it ; the lodger is merely the inmate.  Whenever that happens the lodging-house keeper is rateable, although the lodger is the person in possession ; and although he would have a good

*Watkins v. Milton-next-Gravesend.*

---

[1] *Watkins* v. *Milton-next-Gravesend*, L. R. 3 Q. B. 350 ; 37 L. J. M. C. 73.

[2] *R.* v. *Trent and Mersey Naviga-* tion *Co.*, 3 L. J. (O. S.) K. B. 140 ; 4 B. & C. 57.

[3] L. R. 3 Q. B. 350 ; 37 L. J. M. C. 73.

action against the landlord if he were to put another lodger
in occupation with him."

Whether there is rateable possession or not, is a question Whether
of fact, depending on the circumstances existing in each possession,<br>a question of
instance, but the decided cases may be usefully referred to fact.
for suggestions of the tests that have from time to time been
applied to determine who is the party in possession as well
as for illustration of the general principles above stated.

## I.—POSSESSION OF THE SOIL AS DISTINGUISHED FROM EASEMENT OR LICENSE.

In *R.* v. *Joliffe,*[1] the defendant, for the purpose of R. *v.* Joliffe—
carrying coals from his mines, obtained a lease of wayleaves Wayleave.
or liberties of passage for coal waggons over certain lands,
with liberty to make and lay waggon ways through those
lands. He did not lay down any waggon ways himself, but
used those made by another person who held a similar lease
to his own, paying that person, for the use of the ways, so
much per ton of coals carried. As he made no waggon way
of his own, no soil passed to him under the lease from the
freeholder to himself, which granted to him the soil in such
parts only as he should make a way ; and with regard to his
use of the other person's ways it was held that he had only
a bare right of passage, which was an easement and therefore
not rateable.

In *R.* v. *Churchill,*[2] the burgesses and occupiers of ancient R. *v.* Churchill
messuages within a borough, had, as such, for a portion of —Right of<br>common.
the year, the right to turn cattle into certain fields, and to
exclude during that period the freeholders as well as other
people. It was argued that they were in exclusive occupa-

---

[1] 2 T. R. 90. Cf. *R.* v. *Bell*, page 25, supra.  [2] 4 B. & C. 750 ; 6 Dow. & Ry. 635.

tion, but held that they had no possession of the soil, but only a right of common, and therefore were not rateable.

Watkins v.<br>Milton-next-<br>Gravesend—<br>License to<br>moor.

In *Watkins* v. *Milton-next-Gravesend*,[1] the Conservators of the Thames had granted to the appellant liberty and license to fasten and thenceforth keep fastened his coal hulk to moorings placed by the Conservators in the river, until either party should have given the other one calendar month's notice in writing. In consideration thereof the appellant agreed to pay towards the expense of placing, maintaining and repairing the moorings the annual sum of £30. The moorings belonged to the Conservators, and were laid down in soil which was in their possession, unless the above amounted to a demise of the soil, which it was held it did not, and therefore there was no possession of the soil in the appellant, but only a license to moor, which was not rateable.

Cory v. Bris-<br>tow—Occupa-<br>tion of soil by<br>moorings.

*Watkins* v. *Milton-next-Gravesend* may be compared with *Cory* v. *Bristow*,[2] where the Conservators gave permission to the plaintiff to lay down moorings and moor a derrick hulk to them, subject to a condition that the Conservators might remove the moorings, if it became expedient to do so, on a week's notice. Here the moorings belonged to the plaintiff, and it was held that in respect of them he was in possession of a part of the soil of the bed of the river, and therefore was rateable.

Pimlico<br>Tramway Co.<br>v. Greenwich<br>—Occupation<br>of soil by<br>tram-rails.

In *Pimlico Tramway Co.* v. *Greenwich*,[3] where a tramway company had laid down tram-rails in a highway, under an Act one section of which provided that the Co. were not to acquire any right other than that of user in such highway, it was argued that they had only a right in the nature of a wayleave, but held that they were in possession at all events

---

[1] L. R. 3 Q. B. 350; 37 L. J. M. C. 73.     [3] L. R. 9 Q. B. 9; 43 L. J. M. C. 29.
[2] 2 App. Cas. 262; 46 L. J. M. C. 273.

of the space in the soil de facto filled by their rails, and were therefore rateable. But in *Williams* v. *Jones*[1] it was held that a post, to which ferry boats were sometimes moored, driven into the soil of a highway was not of itself enough to render the ferry rateable. Here however there was apparently nothing to prevent other persons from using it also.

*Williams v. Jones.*

If a railway company have 'running powers' over the line of another company, the former company are not rateable in the parishes where that condition of things exists, because they are only in the enjoyment of an easement there, not in occupation of the soil.[2]

Railway Co.—Running powers.

All the circumstances of the case must be taken into consideration in determining whether a particular person is in possession or not.

All the circumstances to be taken into consideration.

In some cases stress has been laid on ability or otherwise to maintain trespass, as ability to maintain trespass also depends on actual and exclusive possession. In *Allan* v. *Liverpool* and *Inman* v. *Kirkdale*,[3] Blackburn, J., says, "The poor rate is a rate imposed by the statute on the occupier, and that occupier must be the exclusive occupier, a person who if there was a trespass committed on the premises would be the person to bring an action of trespass for it." In *R.* v. *Watson*,[4] where the corporation of a borough were owners in fee of commonable land which by custom was annually meted out to certain of the burgesses for the purpose of turning out their cattle, those who so used it paying a certain sum to those who did not, and the question was whether the corporation, or the burgesses who stocked the commons were the occupiers, Lord Ellenborough, C. J., and Lawrence, J., in deciding that the burgesses were the occupiers, relied on

Trespass.

---

[1] 12 East 346.
[2] *Midland Ry. Co.* v. *Badgworth*, 34 L. J. M. C. 25; s. c. *R.* v. *Midland Ry. Co.*, 11 L. T. N. S. 303.
[3] L. R. 9 Q. B. 180; 43 L. J. M. C. 69.
[4] 5 East 480.

the fact that they could, and the corporation could not, maintain trespass.   Other cases where ability to maintain trespass has been referred to as a criterion are *R.* v. *Morrish*[1] and *Grant* v. *Oxford Local Board.*[2]

Title,

Although when it is established that possession does exist, it is immaterial whether it is with or without title, and the occupier's title is consequently irrelevant and not to be regarded at all, yet while the question of possession or no possession is still sub judice, title is one of those circumstances upon which as a whole the decision is to be founded.

relevant to explain user consistent with either possession or easement.

Where a user exists, which unexplained, is consistent either with possession or with an interest not amounting to possession, then the title by virtue of which such user exists may be looked to, in order to explain the user, and to ascertain whether it is to be referred to possession or easement.   If a person is de facto in the exclusive enjoyment of an hereditament, he is primâ facie an occupier, but a reference to his title may show that he is merely a licensee.   A person who is ostensibly an occupier may appeal to his title to prove that he is not one in reality.   For instance, in such a case as *Watkins* v. *Milton-next-Gravesend,*[3] supra, page 42, where a person is found making a use of moorings consistent with his being either a lessee in possession of the soil or a mere grantee of a license to moor, then reference is to be made to his title to ascertain in which capacity he is acting.   In *R.* v. *St. Mary Abbott's, Kensington,*[4] the question was whether the purchasers of vaults from a cemetery company incorporated by statute were occupiers, or were only in the enjoyment of an easement.   The form of conveyance used was set out in the statute.   It provided that such conveyance should be sufficient to vest the exclusive right of burial, and inter

---

[1] 32 L. J. M. C. 245.                [3] L. R. 3 Q. B. 350; 37 L. T. M. C. 73.
[2] L. R. 4 Q. B. 9; 38 L. J. M. C. 39.      [4] 10 L. J. M. C. 25; 12 A. & E. 825.

alia prohibited the company from selling any land set apart
for burial.  In deciding that the purchasers took only an
easement, Coleridge, J., said, "Some facts stated in the case
look like an occupation by the purchasers, but they are explained by reference to the statute." In *R.* v. *Alnwick*[1]
the question was whether certain persons were occupiers or
commoners.  They enjoyed a user consistent with either
capacity, but they were held to be commoners, and consequently not rateable, on the ground that the original relation
between them and the owner of the land was that of commoners and lord.  So reference to title may be necessary to
ascertain whether a railway company using a line or a
station are occupiers or are only in the enjoyment of the
license to use commonly called 'running powers.'[2]  See
also *Mildmay* v. *Wimbledon.*[3]

But the mere existence of words of demise or words of
license in the document constituting title will not be conclusive.  The general intention of the parties and the real substance of the transaction are to be looked to in preference
to any mere isolated words or expressions.  In *Smith* v. *St.
Michael, Cambridge,*[4] which was recognised and followed in
*R.* v. *St. Pancras,*[5] Hill and Blackburn, JJ., in holding an
agreement not to be a demise, in spite of the words "agrees
to let," "possession to be given," and "rent to commence,"
said "we think that we must look not so much at the words
as the substance of the agreement."  But it must be remembered that what the parties intended to do is only
relevant while it is yet undetermined what they have
done.  In *Allan* v. *Liverpool* and *Inman* v. *Kirkdale,*[6]

*Substance of agreement more important than mere words.*

[1] 8 L. J. M. C. 50; 9 A. & E. 444.
[2] *Midland Ry. Co.* v. *Badgworth,*
34 L. J. M. C. 25; s. c. *R.* v. *Midland
Ry. Co.,* 11 L. T. N. S. 303.
[3] 41 L. J. M. C. 133.

[4] 30 L. J. M. C. 74; 3 E. & E.
383.
[5] 2 Q. B. D. 581; 46 L. J. M. C. 243.
[6] L. R. 9 Q. B. 180; 43 L. J. M.
C. 69.

Allan *v.* Liverpool, and Inman *v.* Kirkdale.

where the appellants were owners of steamships using certain quay space, sheds, &c., in the Mersey Docks, appropriated to their use in a letter from the Dock Board, Blackburn, J., said, "It is quite clear that what we have to see is, whether or not the board parted with the exclusive possession of the premises the subject of the rate, to the persons who have been rated, in the one case Messrs. Allan, and in the other Mr. Inman, so as to make them respectively the occupiers in the sense I have stated. In order to ascertain this, we must see what was the intention of the parties, and that depends not so much upon what words may have been used in the documents employed, for the word 'let' may have been used without there being a letting, and the word 'let' may have been carefully avoided, and yet it may appear that in fact the occupation has been parted with. What we have to look at, taking all the circumstances together, is, to see whether or not there was any exclusive occupation parted with by the board to these persons." In *Smith and Son v. Lambeth*[1] the question was whether the appellants were rateable as occupiers of certain portions of railway platforms on which they had placed and maintained bookstalls, or whether they were merely grantees of the privilege of exclusive enjoyment. The title of the appellants consisted in an indenture made between them and the railway company. Whether this indenture was a demise or a license was the test of their rateability or otherwise. Field, J., said, "The company have granted something. What was it? Was it exclusive occupation or exclusive enjoyment? Have they parted with the occupation? To determine this we must look at the whole scope of the agreement."[2]

Smith and Son *v.* Lambeth.

---

[1] 9 Q. B. D. 585 ; 51 L. J. M. C. 106 ; affirmed C. A., 10 Q. B. D. 327 ; 52 L. J. M. C. 1.

[2] See also per Cairns, L. C., in *Cory* v. *Bristow*, 2 App. Cas. 262, at 275 ; 46 L. J. M. C. 273.

Among the circumstances that have been taken into con-  Repair
sideration in determining whether a person is or is not in
possession is his liability to repair, since primâ facie the
person liable to repair is the person in possession. But
liability to repair is not more than primâ facie evidence.[1]

Another circumstance relevant to the question of license  Rates and
or demise is payment of rates and taxes. If the owner of  taxes.
land is to pay them that is evidence that his intention was
not to create a tenancy, but to grant only a license.[2]

## II.—FREEDOM FROM THE CONTROL OF A PARAMOUNT OCCUPATION IN A SUPERIOR.

The original occupier may grant away something which  Paramount
appears like the occupation, but if he retains to himself a  occupation
right of (a) entry on, or (b) general control over the property,
he retains to himself a paramount occupation and is still
rateable, or rather it would be more correct to say that, if he
has made such a reservation, he has not parted with the possession, but has granted only the exclusive enjoyment of it.
A grantee who has not the right of excluding the grantor is
not in rateable occupation.

In R. v. Morrish,[3] the Royal Commissioners of the Exhibi-  (a) Right of
tion of 1862 allotted to the appellant (a refreshment con-  entry.
tractor), a certain space within the Exhibition building, for
the purpose of selling refreshments. In accordance with his
agreement with the Commissioners he entered on this space,
made cellars, laid on gas and water and sold refreshments
there, but it was held that he had no such occupation as

---

[1] Per Blackburn, J. in *Watkins* v.
*Milton-next-Gravesend*, L. R. 3 Q. B.
350; 37 L. T. M. C. 73; see also
*Cory* v. *Bristow*, 2 App. Cas. 262;
46 L. J. M. C. 273; *R.* v. *St. Mary
Abbott's, Kensington*, 10 L. J. M. C.
25; 12 A. & E. 824, and *R.* v. *Abney
Park Cemetery Co.*, L. R. 8 Q. B.
515; 42 L. J. M. C. 124.
[2] *Mogg* v. *Yatton*, 50 L. J. M. C.
17; 29 W. R. 74.
[3] 32 L. J. M. C. 245.

would render him rateable, because he had no right to exclude the Commissioners. Wightman, J., said, "To make the occupier liable the occupation ought to be exclusive in its nature. Here the appellant could hardly have power to turn off the Commissioners and their friends, if they had chosen to walk through the 40,000 square feet of the Exhibition premises which had been appropriated to him with the exclusive privilege of selling refreshments. The Commissioners would have a right to walk over that part, leaving to the appellant his exclusive privilege of selling refreshments. It seems to me that there was a mere grant of the license to exercise the right of supplying refreshments within the space allotted to him, and for the purpose of exercising that right to make certain erections, but that there was no such occupation as would make him liable to pay rates."

(b) General control.

In *Allan* v. *Liverpool* and *Inman* v. *Kirkdale*,[1] where certain quay space in the Mersey Docks was set apart by the Dock Board for the use of the steamers of a particular owner, he was held not rateable on the ground that the Dock Board (exercising as they did statutable powers of regulating to some extent the use of the quays by imposing a penal rent for goods left lying upon them) retained a general control over the docks. So where the corporation of a borough are seised in fee of pasture lands, to the actual enjoyment of which, the burgesses or certain of them are entitled, then if the corporation exercise a general management or control by a ranger,[2] or a pasture-master,[3] the burgesses are not in rateable occupation. In *R.* v. *St. Mary Abbott's, Kensington*,[4] the Cemetery Co. case referred to supra on page 44, Denman, C. J., says, "The Company are occupiers of the whole premises. The cemetery is under their control and superintendence " . . . . and

[1] L. R. 9 Q. B. 180; 43 L. J. M. C. 69.    C. 121; 6 A. & E. 419. Cf. *R.* v. *Sterry*,
[2] *R.* v. *Sudbury*, 1 B. & C. 389.    9 L. J. M. C. 195; 12 A. & E. 84.
[3] *R.* v. *York (Mayor of)*, 6 L. J. M.    [4] 10 L. J. M. C. 25; 12 A. & E. 824.

Williams, J. :—"No doubt the Company are in the occupation of the whole cemetery. They have the regulation and the repair of it, and the general superintendence over it. They have the control of the external entrance." In *Smith & Son* v. *Lambeth*,[1] where it was sought to rate the appellants as occupiers of bookstalls maintained by them on railway platforms under an agreement with the Railway Co., Cave, J. said, "The persons they employ are to be under the control of the station-master. They are thus controlled in their access, in the mode of enjoyment, and in respect of the persons employed by them at the several stations. How then can it be said that they are tenants having exclusive legal occupation of the premises?" In *L. & N. W. Ry. Co.* v. *Buckmaster*,[2] the defendant was in use, under an agreement, of stables belonging to a Railway Co. The stables were situated within the curtilage of one of the Company's stations. It was contended that the agreement amounted to a demise and passed the possession to the defendant, but on the strength of a clause by which the defendant agreed to observe, and be bound by, any bye-laws the Company might make for the government of their stations and premises, it was held in the Court of Queen's Bench[3] that the Company retained a power of general control in consequence of which the defendant was not in rateable occupation.

This case is an authority for the proposition that a mere power of control is sufficient without any control being actually exercised; for the Company had not in fact exercised

*Or mere power of control, although not exercised.*

---

[1] 9 Q. B. D. 585 ; 51 L. J. M. C. 106 ; affirmed C. A., 10 Q. B. D. 327 ; 52 L. J. M. C. 1.

[2] L. R. 10 Q. B. 70, and on appeal L. R. 10 Q. B. 444 ; 44 L. J. M. C. 180.

[3] On appeal the Court of Exchequer Chamber was equally divided, Lord Coleridge, C.J. and Pollock and Amphlett, B.B., being of opinion that the judgment of the Court below should be affirmed, and Cleasby, B., and Grove and Denman, J.J., holding that on the facts the stable was a separate tenement, and that the agreement operated as a demise.

any control over the stables or made any bye-laws applicable to them.[1]

Pew-renter.

If churches and chapels were at the present day subject to poor rates, pew-renters would not be rateable occupiers. In *Stocks* v. *Booth*,[2] Buller, J., says, "Trespass will not lie for entering into a pew, because the plaintiff has not the exclusive possession, the possession of the church being in the parson;" and in *R.* v. *Agar*[3] (previous to the exemption of churches and chapels), the trustees of a chapel, and not the pew-renters, were rated as occupiers of the pews although in one instance[4] the lessee of a private box at a theatre was held to be rateable: but that was as the occupier of a "tenement" within 10 Geo. III. c. 75, a local Act.

Innkeeper.

A guest at an inn has the right to exclusive possession of his rooms as against strangers; and as against the innkeeper also, with the sole exception that the innkeeper is entitled to enter by himself or his servants for such purposes as are manifestly implied in the relation of innkeeper and guest, such as lighting fires, bringing in meals, and other services of that description. The innkeeper has parted with the right of the exclusive enjoyment of the occupation, but the qualified right of entry and the general control which he exercises, amount to a retaining of possession and render him the rateable occupier.[5]

Lodger.

So also the landlord of a lodger, though not rendering services like the innkeeper, yet is the rateable occupier if he retains dominion and control over the building as a whole. As to what amounts to such dominion and control, Cockburn, C. J., says: [6] "It is necessary to establish some criterion, and it

---

[1] Per Amphlett B., L. R. 10 Q. B. at 446; 44 L. J. M. C. at 181.

[2] 1 T. R. 430.

[3] 14 East 256.

[4] *R.* v. *St. Martin's-in-the-Fields*,

11 L. J. M. C. 112; 3 Q. B. 204.

[5] *Smith* v. *St. Michael, Cambridge*, 30 L. J. M. C. 74; 3 E. & E. 383.

[6] In *R.* v. *St. George's Union*, L. R. 7 Q. B. 90; 41 L. J. M. C. 30.

is not always perhaps very easy to find one; but the one
which has been adopted in such cases, and which is, perhaps,
the most convenient and the only one, is, whether the landlord retains the control of the outer door, and has shown, by
his retaining the control of the outer door, that he has the
control of the whole of the premises; so that although he
may be liable to an action upon the breach of his contract to
allow the tenant to occupy a portion of the premises so let to
the tenant, yet the tenant could not maintain trespass against
the landlord, because the landlord has retained in himself
the dominion and control over the whole of the house. I
think the possession of the street door may be taken as a
criterion, because it is only by the landlord opening and
shutting the street door, or allowing it to be opened and shut
for the ingress and egress of the tenant, that the tenant can
have the enjoyment of the premises."

Another illustration of exclusive enjoyment without pos- Cabin
session, somewhat similar to that of a guest at an inn, is that passenger.
of a passenger who hires a separate cabin for himself in a
ship; and, indeed, if a man hired a whole ship the possession
would remain in the owner so long as she was navigated by
a captain and crew in the owner's employ.[1]

As a lodger is not rateable on account of the paramount Servant,
occupation of the landlord, so one who resides in another's
house as his servant is not rateable. The servant has the
use of the rooms, but has no occupation distinct from, and
independent of, that of his master, and the occupation of a
servant *as servant*, is in law the occupation of the master,
and the master is the rateable occupier. In *R.* v. *Tynemouth*,[2] where it was attempted to rate a man who resided
in a lighthouse as servant of the owner, his duty being to
take care of the light, Lord Ellenborough, C. J., held that the

---

[1] *Dean* v. *Hogg & Lewis*, 10 Bing.     [2].12 East 46.
345.

occupation was clearly that of the master, by his servant, and not that of the servant himself.[1]

occupying as *servant* not rateable. But it is not always clear whether a person does occupy as servant or as tenant. A person may be a servant and yet not occupy *as servant*. It is laid down by Mellor, J., in *Smith* v. *Seghill*,[2] as follows : " Where the occupation is necessary for the performance of services, and the occupier is required to reside in the house in order to perform those services, the occupation being strictly ancillary to the performance of the duties which the occupier has to perform, the occupation is that of a servant."

Examples. For example, the coachman who is placed in rooms over the stable, the gardener who is put into a house in the garden, the gatekeeper who resides in the lodge at a park gate, whose habitations are allotted to them for, and whose occupation conduces to, the better performance of their duties, occupy as servants.[3]

Where both the conditions mentioned by Mellor, J., in *Smith* v. *Seghill*, supra, exist, there is no doubt that the occupation is as servant ; but the existence of either one by itself would appear to be sufficient, and the rule for distinguishing occupation as servant from occupation as tenant Rule for distinguishing occupation as servant from occupation as tenant. may be stated thus :—The occupation is as servant, either (1), if it is reasonably necessary for, or if it substantially facilitates, the better performance of the duties of the service ; or (2), if it is required by the employer with a view to the better performance of those duties.

In *Fox* v. *Dalby*,[4] Coleridge, C. J., says: "As is well pointed out by Cresswell, J., and Crowder, J., in *Clarke* v. *Overseers*

---

[1] Other authorities are *R.* v. *Terrott*, 3 East 506, per Lord Ellenborough C. J. at 514 ; *R.* v. *Aberystwith*, 10 East 354 ; *R.* v. *St. Mary the Less, Durham*, 4 T. R. 477 ; *R.* v. *S. Field*, 5 T. R. 587.

[2] L. R. 10 Q. B. 422 ; 44 L. J. M. C. 114.

[3] *Dobson* v. *Jones*, 13 L. J. C. P. 126 ; 5 M. & G. 112.

[4] L. R. 10 C. P. 285 ; 44 L. J. C. P. 42.

*of Bury St. Edmunds,*[1] if either ingredient exists—if the occupation be necessary for the better performance of the duties required to be performed by the party, or if, though it be not necessary for their performance, he is required by the authority by which he is appointed to reside there in order to perform them—the occupation is not an occupation as tenant." And Brett, J., says, "the principle by which the Court has been guided in dealing with this question is fully stated in *Hughes* v. *Overseers of Chatham,*[2] as explained and enforced in *Dobson* v. *Jones,*[3] and further illustrated by the case of *Clarke* v. *Overseers of Bury St. Edmunds.*[4] The result of those three cases seems to be this, that where a person situate like the respondent is permitted (allowed, if so minded) to occupy premises by way of reward for his services, or as part payment, his occupation is that of tenant ; but that where he is required to occupy them for the better performance of his duties, though his residence there is not necessary for that purpose, or, if his residence there be

---

[1] 26 L. J. C. P. 12 ; 1 C. B. N. S. 23.

[2] 13 L. J. C. P. 44 ; 5 M. & G. 54.

[3] 13 L. J. C. P. 126 ; 5 M. & G. 112.

[4] 26 L. J. C. P. 12 ; 1 C. B. N. S. 23. The nature of the three cases referred to by Brett, J., was as follows :—In *Hughes* v. *Chatham,* a master rope-maker in a royal dock-yard occupied, as such, a house in the dockyard, but his occupation being granted in payment of services, rather than for the purpose of performing them, was held to be occupation as tenant and not as servant. In *Dobson* v. *Jones,* a house in the infirmary of a hospital was assigned to the hospital surgeon, and it was one of the regulations of the hospital that all the officers were to inhabit the apartments assigned to them. Held that, having regard to the nature of his duties, he was required to occupy with a view to their better performance, and consequently occupied as servant. In *Clarke* v. *Bury St. Edmunds (Overseers of),* the hall-keeper of the Guildhall of the borough occupied an adjoining house that was specially built as a hall-keeper's residence. It was admitted that the occupation was part of the remuneration of his services, but that did not prevent it from being occupation as servant, because as he was required to occupy for the better performance of his duties, the second test was satisfied.

necessary for the performance of his duties, though not specifically required, his occupation is not that of tenant."

With regard to the requirement of residence by the employer, Mellor, J., says, in *Smith* v. *Seghill*, supra, " 'Required' means more than the master saying, 'You must reside in one of my houses if you come into my service.' The residence must be ancillary and necessary to the performance of the servant's duties ; and unless he is required *for that purpose* to reside in the house, and not merely as an arbitrary regulation on the part of the master, I do not think he is prevented from occupying as a tenant." Reading this in connection with the other cases, it appears that the principle to be collected from them is that a mere requirement by the master is not enough of itself to determine that the occupation is as servant, if the motive of the master in making it, is any other than desire for the better performance of the service. It sometimes happens that a master requires a servant to occupy, not with any view to the better performance of the service, but because it suits the master to utilise a house or a room by making the occupation of it pass for payment or part payment of the services rendered : an occupation in obedience to a requirement dictated by a motive such as this would be occupation as tenant. Cresswell, J., says, in *Clarke* v. *Bury St. Edmunds (Overseers of)*,[1] "It is true that he " (the occupier) " may occupy as tenant, and yet may be required to occupy. For instance, a man might say to another, 'I will take you as my servant provided you occupy that house and pay me so much a year for it.' The question is whether he occupies as servant ; and if he is required to occupy, whether he is required to do so in the capacity of a servant." In other words, is the residence part of the contract of service, or is it a condition precedent to the contract ?

---

[1] 26 L. J. C. P. 12 ; 1 C. B. N. S. 23.

Given that a servant is required to occupy, the next question is, Is the occupation by way of payment for services or for the purpose of performing them ? The fact that a house is granted in part payment for services is not enough to make the occupation auxiliary to the service.[1] It will not be occupation as servant in accordance with test (1), (supra, page 52,) unless it is for the purpose of performing the services ; but if the requirement may reasonably be referred to that motive, then it will be immaterial to show that in fact the service could be equally well performed from another residence, or that the occupation, although required for the purpose of performing services, is also treated as part payment for them.

In *Fox* v. *Dalby*,[2] the Commanding Officer of a regiment of militia assigned to a sergeant, whose duty it was to look after the arms, &c. of the regiment, a house close to the premises in which the arms were stored. He could have performed his duties if living elsewhere, but had he left the house without the permission of the Commanding Officer he would have been guilty of a breach of discipline, for which he would probably have been dismissed from the Service. It was held that he occupied as a servant, by Coleridge, C. J., Brett and Denman, J.J., all of whom considered that the facts of the case showed that it was with a view to the better performance of his duties that the Commanding Officer required him to live in that house. *Cases on occupation as servant:—*  *Fox v. Dalby.*

In *Smith* v. *Seghill*,[3] some colliery owners allotted certain cottages free of rent to the colliers in their employ, giving preference to the married men. The occupation of those cottages was not a compulsory incident of the service, (as in the case of the militia sergeant in *Fox* v. *Dalby*, supra), and a *Smith v. Seghill.*

---

[1] *R.* v. *Wall Lynn*, 8 A. & E. 379.    [3] L. R. 10 Q. B. 422 ; 44 L. J. M.
[2] L. R. 10 C. P. 285 ; 44 L. J. C.    C. 114.
P. 42.

refusal to reside would not have involved dismissal, but only the loss of an allowance which was made to men whose turn had not come for the offer of a cottage, apparently to compensate them for having to reside at a distance. It was stated that the owners preferred that the colliers should live near their work, but it was not necessary for them to live in cottages belonging to the owners to enable them to perform it. The occupation being neither necessary for their duties, nor compulsory, it was held to be the occupation of tenants, Mellor, J., saying, "The colliery owners desire that the married workmen should reside near the works, but that does not change the relation between the parties; unless the men are required to live in the houses for the better performance of their duties, it does not convert the occupation of a tenant into that of a servant. The governing principle is that in order to constitute an occupation as a servant, it must be an occupation ancillary to the performance of the duties which the occupier has engaged to perform. Here the occupation is not connected with the performance of the employment, and the appellants therefore occupy as tenants."

R. v. S. Field.    In *R. v. S. Field*,[1] a society, which maintained a home for the care and education of the children of convicts, employed a person as superintendent of the home, under agreement that she should, inter alia, have " a dwelling free from taxes." It was argued that she occupied as tenant, because she was in fact the head of, and had control over, the house; but on the other hand she was placed in the house for the express purpose of superintending it, which was the service she was engaged to perform, and it was held that she occupied as servant.

R. v. Catt.    *R. v. Catt*,[2] where a schoolmaster was held rateable for

---

[1] 5 T. R. 587; cf. *R. v. Waldo*,    [2] 6 T. R. 332.
Cald. 358.

a house with garden and orchard, which he held as master of
the school, is not inconsistent with *R.* v. *S. Field,* supra. The
house, garden, and orchard were assigned by deed " for the
use of him and his family " without payment of rent. The
garden and orchard at all events, were not connected with his
duties, and as to the house, the circumstances pointed rather
to an occupation beneficial to himself, granted by way of
part payment for his services, than to a mere being put in to
look after the pupils. Here, as in *R.* v. *Minster,*[1] something
was given to the servant unconnected with the service,
which therefore he could not be said to occupy as servant.

The distinction between the two last mentioned cases and R. *v.* Shepherd.
*R.* v. *Shepherd,*[2] where the governor of a gaol, obliged to live
within the walls, was held not rateable for the house he
occupied, is that there it was found as a fact that the accommodation provided for him was such only as, and no more
than, was necessary for his convenient accommodation.

But even where a person occupies as a servant, so soon as
independent occupation, ultra the service and for private advantage, is discovered, then rateability attaches to him.[3]

The first test (see page 52, supra,) seems to meet the case
of a contractor occupying land for the purpose of carrying
out a contract to do something to it or upon it.[4]

It was admitted in argument in *R.* v. *Gardner,*[5] and was R. *v.* Gardner
decided in *R.* v. *Wall Lynn,*[6] that the College butler and Lynn.
porter in the former case, and the servant Lynn in the latter,
occupied as tenants, on the ground that their occupation was
free from paramount control by their respective masters.

---

[1] 3 M. & S. 276 ; cf. *R.* v. *Cheshunt,* 1 B. & Ald. 473.

[2] 10 L. J. M. C. 44 ; 1 Q. B. 170.

[3] *Bristol* v. *Wait,* 5 L. J. M. C. 113 ; 5 A. & E. 1 ; *R.* v. *Terrott,* 3 East 506 ; *Bute* v. *Grindall,* 1 T. R. 338 ; *R.* v. *Stewart,* 27 L. J. M. C.

81 ; 8 E. & B. 360 ; *R.* v. *Ponsonby,* 11 L. J. M. C. 65 ; 3 Q. B. 14 ; *R.* v. *Bridgehouse,* 20 L. T. N. S. 658.

[4] See *Tyne Coal Co.* v. *Wallsend,* 46 L. J. M. C. 185.

[5] Cowp. 78.

[6] 8 A. & E. 379.

### III.—POSSESSION THAT IS SOLE AND EXCLUSIVE.

*Possession must be sole and exclusive,*

To constitute such possession as will form an element of rateability, there must be not only, in the first place, possession as distinguished from easement or license, and secondly, freedom from paramount occupation, but also, thirdly, possession that is sole and exclusive as against all the world.

In *Grant* v. *Oxford Local Board*,[1] it was sought to rate the University Boat Club for a barge which had been for twenty years moored to two posts driven into the bed of the river; but it was held that there was no rateable occupation on their part, since it did not appear that they could prevent other persons from also attaching their barges or boats to the posts.

*of even possible co-grantees.*

Whatever rights and privileges over land may have been granted by the owner to any person, that person will not be a rateable occupier if the owner has the power of granting similar rights and privileges to others.

*R. v. Trent and Mersey Navigation Co.*

For example, in *R.* v. *Trent and Mersey Navigation Co.*,[2] the owners of a quarry contracted to supply the defendant Company yearly and every year for ever, at a certain price, with as much stone as they should think fit to order; and it was provided that if they should neglect to do so, the Company might enter upon the quarry and work the stone for themselves, paying the owners a certain sum for every ton they so worked. The owners having neglected to supply the stone ordered, the Company entered, and for more than twenty years worked the quarry for themselves, and no one else ever had in fact got stone there. But it was held that the Company were not in rateable occupation, because they had no power of excluding any other persons to whom the owners might grant similar privileges. Abbott, C. J., said that " the

---

[1] L. R. 4 Q. B. 9 ; 38 L. J. M. C. 39.    [2] 3 L. J. K. B. 140 ; 4 B. & C. 57.

right of the Company was merely to get there what stone
they might think fit; there was nothing in the contract to
prevent the owner from giving to others also the privilege
of getting stone in the same quarry. The Company, therefore, had not any sole and exclusive occupation, but a mere
privilege, and consequently were not liable to be rated to the
relief of the poor."

In *R.* v. *Tewkesbury*,[1] the aftermath of a certain meadow
was vested in trustees for the burgesses and principal householders of a borough. The trustees let out the pasture to
various persons at so much per head of cattle. These persons
failed to be rateable occupiers because there was nothing to
prevent the trustees from taking in also the cattle of others.

    *R. v. Tewkes-bury,*

The distinction between this case and *R.* v. *Watson* (supra,
page 43), is that there the number of burgesses privileged to
stock the commonable land was fixed and ascertained, and the
corporation could not take in the cattle of a stranger. That
being so, it was held that the burgesses entitled to stock were
tenants in common, and rateable.

    *distinguished from R. v. Watson.*

In cases such as those above mentioned, if the grantee
is not rateable, the grantor is; they cannot each succeed in
clearing themselves from rateability. If the grantee can
establish that he has not been clothed with exclusive possession, then the grantor has not parted with the occupation.
One of them is rateable; the question is, which one.

    *If grantee not a rateable occupier the grantor is.*

The rule that sole and exclusive possession is essential to
rateability does not, of course, discharge those who occupy
an undivided property as tenants in common or joint
tenants.

    *Tenants in common and joint tenants.*

---

[1] 13 East 155.

## ACTUAL USER.

There must be some actual user, though a small amount is sufficient.

The second essential of rateable occupation is some amount, at least, of actual user. Mere legal possession is not sufficient of itself, but to constitute rateability, the person entitled to the possession must in addition take some measures, however slight, to make the land beneficial to himself.

To take the example given by Lush, J., in the judgment already quoted,[1] where he says, " the owner of a vacant house is in possession and may maintain trespass against any one who invades it, but so long as he leaves it vacant he is not rateable for it as an occupier. If, however, he furnishes it,[2] and keeps it ready for habitation whenever he pleases to go it, he is an occupier, though he may not reside in it one day in the year ; "—if the owner did not keep the furniture in the house he would have to keep it somewhere else, and he may therefore be regarded as making use of the house, at least as a warehouse for the furniture. Slight as such user may be, it is enough when added to legal possession to constitute occupation.

In *Staley* v. *Castleton*,[3] the owner of a cotton mill which, through a temporary scarcity of cotton, was not kept at work, was held to be in rateable occupation, on the ground that he was using the mill as a warehouse for the machinery that was in it. In such cases the amount of the assessment should, of course, be calculated with reference to the nature of the occupation. A building found to be occupied as a warehouse should be assessed at its value as a warehouse, and not at what its value would be if used as a dwelling house or for any other purpose.

---

[1] Page 37, supra.
[2] *Staunton* v. *Powell*, 1 Ir. R., C. L. 182—Exch. Cham.

[3] 33 L. J. M. C. 178 ; 5 B. & S. 505. Followed in *Harter* v. *Salford*, 34 L. J. M. C. 206 ; 6 B. & S. 591.

Whether an owner is to be rateable at all or not rests en- User of a part
tirely with himself.   If he likes to abstain from any user of a house renders the
whatever of his property, to let his house remain empty or his whole rateable,
lands lie barren, he keeps himself free from rateability.[1] But
if he occupies at all he has no power, by limiting his user to
a part only of the property, to limit correspondingly his rateability.   Actual user in respect of one room is sufficient to
convert legal possession into rateable occupation in respect of
the whole house.

In *R.* v. *St. Mary the Less, Durham,*[2] where the owner of
a house contended that he ought to be rated for two rooms
only, Lord Kenyon, C. J., said, "It would be attended with
great inconvenience to draw such a line as has been attempted
in this case, between the occupation of one part of a house
and that of another." Ashhurst, J. :—"It would be a very in-
convenient practice to inquire in each particular case, what
rooms of a house the owner occupied, before he could be
rated." Grose, J. :—" I consider the appellant as the occupier
of the whole house.   If a person were to shut up his garrets,
it would be no ground to exempt him from being rated for
the whole house."

And in *R.* v. *Aberystwith,*[3] Lord Ellenborough, C. J., said,
" There is no instance where a man has been permitted to
carve out the occupation of his house in the manner now
attempted; locking up one room and then another, but

---

[1] There is however a dictum of
Crompton, J., in *Harter* v. *Salford,*
34 L. J. M. C. 206 ; 6 B. & S. 591, to
the effect that a landlord who has the
opportunity of letting at a fair rent,
and declines to let, is to be rated though
the house remains empty ; but contra,
and in support of the text, see *R.* v.
*St. Luke's Hospital* (overruling *Anon.*
2 Salk. 527) 2 Burr. 1053 ; *Kempe*
v. *Spence,* 2 Wm. Bl. 1244 ; *R.* v.

*Morgan,* 2 A. & E. 618 n.; s. c. *R.* v.
*Bucks (Justices of)* 3 N. & M. 68 ; *R.*
v. *Malden,* L. R. 4 Q. B. 326 ; 38
L. J. M. C. 125 ; *R.* v. *St. Pancras*
(per Lush, J.), 1 Q. B. D. 581 ; 46 L.
J. M. C. 243 ; and the recognition
of the non-rateability of unoccupied
houses in 32 & 33 Vict. c. 41, sec. 4,
sub-s. 2.
[2] 4 T. R. 477.
[3] 10 East 354.

using as much of the house as he found convenient. This. would make a new system of occupation by sub-divisions."

**but it is not necessary that the same person should be rated for the whole :**

Although a man who is rated for a whole house cannot discharge himself as to part by showing that he is only in actual user of a portion of the house, and that there is no user of the remainder by any one, yet he may limit his rateability to a part only of the house if he can show that the rest is in the distinct and separate occupation of another person.

**different persons may be rated for distinct parts.**

In *R.* v. *Ponsonby*,[1] Patteson, J., says, " I am not aware that the Statute of Elizabeth has ever been held to mean that the same party must be rated for the whole of a house. On the contrary, the cases seem to show that there may be a rating for a part only. In *Ayr* v. *Smallpeace*,[2] the Comptroller of Chelsea College was held rateable for having apartments distinctly and separately to his use. So, from *R.* v. *St. Mary the Less, Durham*,[3] it appears that different persons may be rated for distinct parts of a house. A house, therefore, may be divided into several different holdings."

## TITLE IMMATERIAL.

**Title immaterial if possession exists in fact.**

Although, as has already been pointed out,[4] the amount of title a person possesses, is a relevant fact when the question to be decided is whether he is or is not in possession, yet if he is found to be as a matter of fact in exclusive possession, it is then immaterial whether he has any title or not.

**R. v. Bell.**

In *R.* v. *Bell*[5] the defendant obtained from the Dean and Chapter of Durham (under local circumstances similar to those that existed in *R.* v. *Joliffe*, supra, page 41), a lease

---

[1] 11 L. J. M. C. 65 ; 3 Q. B. 14.     [3] 4 T. R. 477.
[2] 1 Nolan P. L. 154 ; 1 Bott.     [4] Page 44.
P. L. 131 n.                       [5] 7 T. R. 598.

of wayleaves, over certain lands in the occupation of tenants
to whom the Dean and Chapter had already demised them,
with the reservation to themselves of power to make or
grant waggon-ways over them.    The defendant laid down
waggon-ways, and fenced them in, in such a manner as to
keep off them the lessees of the Dean and Chapter as well as
all other persons.    It was held that the defendant was as a
matter of fact clearly in exclusive possession of the soil so
enclosed, and that therefore it was immaterial that he had
no title to more than a wayleave.  .Lord Kenyon, C. J., said,
" One ground of argument is, that because the Dean and
Chapter could only grant a wayleave, therefore nothing more
than a wayleave passed to the defendants, but we are not
to inquire into the titles of the occupiers.  If a disseisor
obtain possession of land, he is rateable as the occupier of it."

So in *Cory* v. *Bristow*,[1] Cairns, L. C., said, "They " (the appellants) " are found in occupation of that which is to them a valuable occupation of this fixed property, and are therefore rateable to the relief of the poor, even though it might turn out that their occupation is a wrongful one, or one the propriety of which they cannot justify."   See also the separate judgments of Blackburn, J., Mellor, J., and Lush, J., in *Kittow* v. *Liskeard Union*.[2]

Cory v. Bris-<br>tow.

A gas or water company which possesses mains buried in the soil is thereby de facto in possession of the space in the soil which the mains fill.   In *R.* v. *West Middlesex Waterworks Co.*,[3] Wightman, J., says, "The decisions are uniform in holding gas companies to be rateable in respect of their mains, although the occupation of such mains may be de facto merely, and without any legal or equitable estate in the land where the mains lie, by force of some statute."

R. v. Middle-<br>sex Water-<br>works.

[1] 2 App. Cas. 262 ; 46 L. J. M.        C. 23.
C. 273.                                [3] 28 L. J. M. C. 135; 1 E. & E.
[2] L. R. 10 Q. B. 7 ; 44 L. J. M.      716.

## PERMANENCE.

Permanence. A third essential of rateable occupation is that it should be of a permanent character.

In *R.* v. *St. Pancras,*[1] Mellor, J., said, "I agree with the opinion cited by Lord Hatherley in *Cory* v. *Bristow,*[2] as that of Lord Campbell, C. J., in the case of *Forrest* v. *Overseers of Greenwich,*[3] viz., that in order to be rateable the occupation must be permanent in its nature. The word 'permanent' may not appear in every one of the judgments delivered at various times, as a description of the kind of occupation necessary, but in the particular cases where no reference is made to the quality of permanence as being a necessary element the facts spoke for themselves with regard to this point." Lush, J.: "Another element, however, besides actual possession of the land, is necessary to constitute the kind of occupation which the Act contemplates, and that is permanence."

It is difficult to frame a definition or to lay down a test of permanence that will meet all cases, but we will consider it with reference to (I.) Time, and (II.) Place.

### I.—PERMANENCE WITH REFERENCE TO TIME.

I. With reference to time. An example of an occupation which is obviously temporary as opposed to permanent, when the intention of the person occupying is considered, is given by Lush, J., in *R.* v. *St. Pancras*[4] :—"An itinerant showman who erects a temporary structure for his performances may be in exclusive actual possession, and may, with strict grammatical propriety, be said to occupy the ground on which

---

[1] 2 Q. B. D. 581 ; 46 L. J. M. C. 243.

[2] 2 App. Cas. 262 ; 46 L. J. M. C. 273.

[3] 8 E. & B. 890 ; s. c. *R.* v. *Forrest,* 27 L. J. M. C. 96.

[4] 2 Q. B. D. 581 ; 46 L. J. M. C. 243.

his structure is placed, but it is clear that he is not such an occupier as the statute intends. As the poor rate is not made day by day or week by week, but for months in advance, it would be absurd to hold that a person who comes into a parish with the *intention* to remain there a few days or a week only, incurs a liability to maintain the poor for the next six months. Thus, a transient, temporary holding of land is not enough to make the holding rateable. It must be an occupation which has in it the character of permanence ; a holding as a settler, not as a wayfarer." So in *R.* v. *St. Pancras,*[1] the decision that Messrs. Willing had only the temporary use of land on which, with the permission of the owners, they affixed advertisement hoardings, was based on reference to the general intention of the parties.

*Intention relevant.*

But occupation does not fail in permanence merely because the *user is intermittent.* In *Birmingham Canal Navigation Co.* v. *Birmingham,*[2] Cockburn, C. J., said, with regard to an engine-house, the engines in which were actually used on an average only about twenty days in the year, at times dependent on the state of the rainfall, "it is only made available and put to a particular use on certain occasions, or if you like, in certain contingencies, nevertheless, it must always be there; it has a certain value with respect to the land and the buildings upon it, and the machinery permanently attached to it, and in that respect I think it ought to be rated, whether it is used all the year or not."

*Immaterial that user is intermittent.*

An opera house or theatre used only during a season would, by parity of reasoning, be none the less rateable on that account.

Neither does occupation fail to be of a permanent cha-

*Shortness of notice immaterial.*

[1] 2 Q. B. D. 581 ; 46 L. J. M. C. 243.          [2] 19 L. T. N. S. 311.

racter merely on account of the *shortness of the notice* by
which it may be determined.

In *Cory* v. *Bristow*,[1] it was argued that the fact that the
user of the moorings might be determined by the Conservators on a week's notice showed that the persons in enjoyment
of them, were licensees rather than occupiers, but Lord
Hatherley said, "It would be a confusion of ideas to say
that it interferes with the exclusive possession, any more
than a right of re-entry on the part of a landlord in certain given events, could be said to interfere in any way
with the right of the tenant during the time he is holding.
He is in beneficial occupation for a term, though that term
is limited by certain contingencies which may possibly determine his interest at an earlier period;" and Lord
O'Hagan said, "Until that notice was given, the Conservators, if they had ventured to intrude upon them," (the
Messrs. Cory) "would have acted illegally, and been liable to
answer in an action. For the time, and subject to the
conditions, the Messrs. Cory were exclusive occupants, as
completely as if their occupation had been of their own fee
simple estate."

**Tenant at will rateable.**  A tenant at will is a rateable occupier, although his
tenancy is determinable at the will of the owner by a de-
mand of possession.[2]

**II. With reference to place.**

## II.—WITH REFERENCE TO PLACE.

**(a.) There must be occupation of a fixed locality,**

(a.) Occupation not permanent because shifting in locality
—In *R.* v. *Morrison*[3] (explained in *Forrest* v. *Greenwich*
(*Overseers of*)[4]), a floating dock or cradle which floated at

---

[1] 2 App. Cas. 262; 46 L. J. M. C. 273.

[2] *Bute* v. *Grindall*, 1 T. R. 338; *R.* v. *Hurdis*, 3 T. R. 497; *R.* v. *Chelsea Water Works Co.*, 2 L. J. M. C. 98; 5 B. & Ad. 156; *R.* v. *Ponsonby*, 11 L. J. M. C. 65; 3 Q. B. 14.

[3] 22 L. J. M. C. 14; 1 E. & B. 150.

[4] 8 E. & B. 890, at 899; s. c. *R.* v. *Forrest*, 27 L. J. M. C. 96.

high tide and grounded at low tide, and was sometimes taken
further out into deeper water, was held not to be the subject
of rateable occupation, because it had no fixed locality ; but
in *Forrest* v. *Greenwich* (*Overseers of*)[1] it was held that a
pier could not be said to have no locality merely because it
floated at high tide.

In *Spear* v. *Bodmin Union*,[2] stalls in a market-house
were let by the year; the stalls were moveable, and after
being removed when the market-house was used for other
purposes, such as bazaars and concerts, were not necessarily
replaced on the exact spots of ground which they previously
occupied, though they were always arranged in the same
part of the market-house and in the same order relatively
to each other. Under these circumstances it was held that
the occupation of the renters of stalls was not rateable,
because deficient in permanence as regards place, for there was
no occupation of a definite portion of the soil. It also failed
to be rateable because it was not exclusive, for the renters
were entitled to the use of the stalls, only on the fixed days
and hours when the market was held, and they could not
exclude other people from the use of the soil at other times.

But in *R.* v. *Whaddon* (*Overseers of*)[3] "a perpetually shifting" occupation of land was held rateable under circumstances
which, briefly stated, were as follows :—A patent manure
company obtained from the owner of certain lands a grant of
the privilege of entering on the lands and raising the coprolites
one of the terms of the agreement being that after having
done so they should level the surface and restore the top
soil. In the course of their operations the company gradually moved, so to speak, across the land, being always in the
occupation of ten acres, on one-third of which the process of

*but see R. v.
Whaddon
(Overseers of),*

*see above*

---

[1] 8 E. & B. 890 ; s. c. *R.* v. *Forrest,*
27 L. J. M. C. 96.

[2] 49 L. J. M. C. 69 ; 44 J. P. 764.

[3] L. R. 10 Q. B. 230 ; 44 L. J. M.
C. 73.

raising the coprolites was going on, the remaining two-thirds being occupied by them for the purpose of fulfilling their obligation to restore the land to its original condition. But although there was *a constant occupation of ten acres,* the occupation was a *perpetually shifting* one, for the company, as they extended their operations acre by acre in the one direction, abandoned land and restored it to the owner in the other. The company were however held rateable in respect of the occupation of ten acres.

and (*b*) in certain cases attachment to the soil as a fixture.

(*b.*) Occupation not permanent because no attachment to the soil as a fixture—

In certain cases there may be an occupation of a permanent character as regards time, and which also satisfies the conditions of permanence as regards place, in so far that the place occupied is always the same, and yet the occupation may fall short of permanence because there is no attachment to the soil as a fixture. Lush, J., says in *R.* v. *St. Pancras*,[1] " Where the subject of occupation is not a surface area—which is the idea primarily suggested by the phrase ' occupier of land '—but only a small portion of the soil, so much of it as contains a post, a pipe, or a rail, the element of permanence or its absence is shown by the way in which the post, &c., is connected with the soil. . . . . . It would be an abuse of language to say that the owner of a post lying upon the ground is thereby occupier of the ground upon which the post rests, however long it may be there ; but if the post is inserted into the ground, or otherwise so attached to it that it cannot be severed from the land without breaking up the soil, it has become one with the soil, and the owner of the post is thereby occupier of the soil to which it is annexed."

---

[1] 2 Q. B. D. 581 ; 46 L. J. M. C. 243.

## PROFIT.—BENEFICIAL OCCUPATION.

Occupation in order to be rateable must be 'beneficial,' that is, it must produce, or be capable of producing, profit. *Occupation must be beneficial,*

If the occupation is productive, or capable of being so, it is immaterial whether the occupier does or does not benefit by the profit produced. If, for any reason whatever, the profit passes into other hands than those of the occupier, that does not discharge him from rateability. The overseers are not required to follow the produce of the occupation, to ascertain who is ultimately benefited by it. It matters not, for instance, that the occupier may be a bare trustee for the public without any personal interest,[1] or that he may have made such an onerous contract with his landlord that he retains none of the profit for himself.[2] *i.e. productive—though not necessarily profitable.*

The law on this point was settled by the House of Lords, after putting questions to the Judges, in the *Mersey Dock Cases,*[3] where they decided that a person in occupation of valuable property is not exempt from rateability because he occupies merely in a fiduciary character. *Mersey Dock Cases.*

Previously it had been held in several cases that persons who occupied as trustees, and did not personally derive any pecuniary benefit or advantage from the occupation, were not rateable. *The previous view of the law as to bare trustees,*

For instance, in *R.* v. *St. Luke's Hospital,*[4] the trustees of a hospital were held not rateable, because they had no personal pecuniary interest in the occupation. In *R.* v. *Commissioners of Salter's Load Sluice,*[5] Navigation Commissioners were exempted as having a bare trust not coupled with any interest. In *R.* v. *Liverpool Docks (Trustees*

---

[1] *Mersey Dock Cases,* 35 L. J. M. C. 1; 11 H. L. C. 443.

[2] *R.* v. *Parrott,* 5 T. R. 593. See *R.* v. *Vange,* 11 L. J. M. C. 117; 3

Q. B. 242.

[3] 35 L. J. M. C. 1; 11 H. L. C. 443.

[4] 2 Burr. 1053.

[5] 4 T. R. 730.

*of*),[1] following the Salter's Load Sluice Case, a Dock Board, who were bound to maintain docks for the public benefit, and empowered to levy dock dues for the purposes only of defraying the cost of construction and the annual cost of maintenance of the docks, were held not rateable.

overruled by Mersey Dock Cases—

But the *Mersey Dock Cases*[2] overruled these and other similar decisions which are there collected and reviewed by Blackburn, J. and Byles, J.

Lord Westbury, L. C., on beneficial occupation.

Lord Westbury, L. C., said in the *Mersey Dock Cases,* "The questions raised in this appeal depend in a great measure on the inquiry,—What is the occupation of real property which is liable to be rated under the 1st section of the Act of the 43 Eliz. c. 2 ? Independently of the decided cases, several of which are irreconcilable with each other, it would seem to be easy to answer this inquiry ; and having regard to the Parochial Assessment Act, it may be said in answer, that ' occupation to be rateable must be of property yielding, or capable of yielding, a net annual value, that is to say, a clear rent over and above the probable average annual cost of the repairs, insurance, and other expenses, if any, necessary to maintain the property in a state to command such rent.' It is in this sense that I understand the words 'beneficial occupation,' wherever it is said that to support a rate the occupation must be a beneficial one. For on principle it is by no means necessary that the occupation should be beneficial to the occupier. It is sufficient if the property be capable of yielding a clear rent over and above the necessary outgoings."

Lord Cranworth.

Lord Cranworth said, " That the defendants in error are occupiers of lands in the parish of Liverpool cannot be doubted, and so, unless there be something to exempt them,

---

[1] 5 L. J. (O. S.) M. C. 145 ; 7 B. & C. 61.

[2] 35 L. J. M. C. 1 ; 11 H. L. C. 443.

they are rateable. The argument on their behalf has been
that though they are occupiers, their occupation is not a
beneficial occupation ; and the statute, it was contended, contemplated only such an occupation as is beneficial to the
occupier, or to some other person or persons for whose
behoof the occupier is occupying. If by beneficial occupation
is meant any occupation of something valuable, something in
its own nature beneficial to some one, I think it is fair to
consider that word as impliedly included in the statute. It
was not meant to impose the duty of contributing to the
relief of the poor on any one, merely because he might be
the occupier of a barren rock, neither yielding nor capable
of yielding any profit from its occupation. But I can dis-
cover nothing, either in the words or the spirit of the Act,
exempting from liability the occupier of valuable property,
merely because the profits of the occupation are not to be
enjoyed by him, or by any one on whose behalf he is
occupying, but are to be devoted to the benefit of the
public."

Lord Chelmsford said : " If an occupier derives no benefit Lord Chelms-
of any description from his occupation, it forms no part of ford.
the general ability of the parish, but if it is productive
(although not profitable), there is nothing in the Act which
requires the overseers to follow the produce in its subsequent
application. The receipt of it constitutes the visible ability
of the occupier. As was said by Lord Tenterden in *R.* v.
*The Inhabitants of St. Giles', York,*[1] 'If any profit be made,
the application of it, when made, is immaterial as to the
question of rateability' . . . . I am of opinion that under
the words of the 43 Eliz. c. 2, every occupier of a tenement
yielding profit is within the rating clause of the statute,
although the tenement be a public work for the general

---

[1] 1 L. J. M. C. 50 ; 3 B. & Ad. 573.

good of the realm, and the profit be directed to be applied exclusively to its maintenance."

**Immaterial what proportion of the profits is received by the occupier.** If the fact that the whole of the profits pass to some one other than the occupier is immaterial, it would seem to follow as of course that it is immaterial that a part of them does so. But in *R.* v. *Rhymney Railway Co.*,[1] it was contended, it need hardly be said without success, that the sole occupier of wharves was not to be rated on certain wharfage dues constituting a part of the value of the occupation, because, by the contract of tenancy, such dues were reserved to the landlord. On the strength of the *Mersey Dock Cases* it was held in *R.* v. *Sherford*,[2] that in rating a vicar for his tithes no deduction can be made for the expense of a curate.

**Mere capability of producing profit sufficient.** Again, if the judgments in the *Mersey Dock Cases*, did not sufficiently establish that in order to constitute beneficial occupation, it is not necessary that profit should be actually produced, but only that the occupation should be capable of producing profit, there is a decision of the House of Lords in the St. Thomas' Hospital case, *London (Mayor of)* v. *Stratton*,[3] where it was contended that the case of a hospital which receives no remuneration from the patients who use it, and produces nothing in the shape of profit, is thereby distinguishable from such a case as that of the Mersey Docks, where tolls were received for their use. But the House held, without calling for a reply to this argument, that no such distinction existed.

In the two last mentioned cases respectively, the Rhymney Railway Co. and the Governors of St. Thomas' Hospital did not dispute that they were in occupation of the premises, and, therefore, it is hard to see how they could

---

[1] L. R. 4 Q. B. 276 ; 38 L. J.   C. 113.
M. C. 75.                          [3] L. R. 7 H. L. 477 ; 45 L. J. M.
[2] L. R. 2 Q. B. 503 ; 36 L. J. M.   C. 22.

have obtained the exemptions they sought, consistently with
the rule laid down in the statute, that the basis of an occupier's rateability is to be the amount the property would
fetch per annum if let to a hypothetical tenant on certain
defined terms.

Briefly, the rule established by the *Mersey Dock Cases* is,   The general rule.
that, if a person is in occupation of a property which pro-
duces, or is capable of producing profit, he is rateable on
the value of the occupation, no matter whether profits are
actually received or not, or what becomes of them when
received.

An example of property not within the rule, because not   Sewers.
the subject of beneficial occupation, is that of the sewers in
the occupation of the Metropolitan Board of Works.[1]

In *Lincoln (Mayor of) v. Holmes Common (Overseers of),*[2]   Lincoln (Mayor of) v. Holmes Common (Overseers of).
the Corporation of Lincoln were the owners and occupiers of
a common, subject to a right in freemen to depasture cattle,
the exercise of which right exhausted the whole of the
pasturage.    The decision that the Corporation were not rateable under these circumstances may appear at first sight not
to be in accordance with the rule that an occupier does not
cease to be rateable because the profits pass into the hands
of some one else.    But it will be found that the majority of
the Court, Blackburn, J., and Shee, J., (Cockburn, C. J., alone
holding that the Corporation were not rateable), held, not that
the Corporation were not rateable occupiers, but that the rate
ought to be reduced to nothing, because in the then existing
circumstances, the cattle of the freemen being numerous
enough to consume the whole pasturage, the occupation of
the Corporation would be worth nothing to the hypothetical
tenant. The amount of their rateability being measured by the

---

[1] *R. v. Metropolitan Board of Works,* L. R. 4 Q. B. 15 ; 39 L. J. M. C. 24 ; *Metropolitan Board of Works* v. *West Ham,* L. R. 6 Q. B. 193 ; 40 L. J. M. C. 15.
[2] L. R. 2 Q. B. 482; 36 L. J. M. C. 73.

value of the occupation to the hypothetical tenant, would vary inversely with the aggregate number of the cattle of the freemen. If, as Blackburn, J., suggested, the number of freemen were ever reduced, so that the aggregate number of cattle they were entitled to turn on the common would not be enough to eat up all the grass, then there would be a margin of benefit for which the Corporation might get a rent from the hypothetical tenant, and for which, consistently with the judgments of Blackburn, J., and Shee, J., they would be rateable.

The reason the enjoyment of the profits by the freemen was held to operate as a discharge of the Corporation was that it was a legal incident of their occupation, which the Corporation had no option of preventing. It was not by any arrangement or contract made by them, that the profits passed to the freemen; if it had been so the Corporation would not have been exempted.

## THE CROWN NOT A RATEABLE OCCUPIER.

*The Crown not bound by a statute unless named in it,*

The law is primâ facie presumed to be made for subjects only, and it is a well recognised rule that the Crown is not bound by a statute unless named in it.[1]

*and therefore not within the 43 Eliz. c. 2.*

The Crown is not named in the 43 Eliz. c. 2, and therefore when property is occupied by the Crown there is not an occupier within the statute, and therefore no one who can be rated.

*Extent of the exemption of the Crown.*

The exemption from rateability which exists when property is in the occupation of the Crown includes cases where the occupation is that of the servants of the Crown

---

[1] Maxwell on the Interpretation of Statutes, 1st edition, p. 112.

occupying for the purposes of the Crown.[1]  The purposes of
the Crown comprise the carrying on of the Government of
the country, the administration of justice, and the discharge
of such other duties as are theoretically the prerogatives of
the Crown.  Accordingly it has been held that property is
not rateable when occupied for the purposes of the Royal
Army and Navy ;[2] or of the Post Office ;[3] for Assize Courts, or
judges' lodgings ;[4] or for Prisons.[5]

Before the *Mersey Dock Cases* there had been decisions in  The old rule,
which the distinction between occupation for public purposes
and occupation for Crown purposes had not been duly
recognised, and exemptions had been admitted in cases

[1] Per Lord Westbury, L. C., and Lord
Cranworth in the Mersey Dock Cases,
35 L. J. M. C. 1 ; 11 H. L. C. 443.

[2] *Amherst* v. *Sommers*, 2 T. R. 372 ;
*R.* v. *Stewart*, 27 L. J. M. C. 81 ; 8 E. &
B. 360.  But to prevent the hardship
which such exemptions entail on the
other occupiers in the parish, the
23 & 24 Vict. c. 112, which was an
Act to enable lands to be acquired for
the construction of fortifications for
the defence of the realm, provided,
by sec. 33, that such lands should
nevertheless continue rateable to the
extent of their previously existing
value, and similarly the 31 & 32
Vict. c. 110, the Act under which
the Post Office purchased the Tele-
graphs, provided by sec. 22, that all
property acquired under that Act by
the Postmaster-General should nevertheless continue to be rateable to the
extent of its previously existing
value.  However, it appears from
*R.* v. *The Postmaster-General*, 28
L. T. N. S. 337 ; 37 J. P. 196, that
this section is of no effect, as the Act
provides no means of enforcing the
payment.

[3] *Smith* v. *Birmingham (Guardians
of)*, 26 L. J. M. C. 105 ; 7 E. & B. 483.

[4] *R.* v. *St. Martin's, Leicester*,
L. R. 2 Q. B. 493 ; 36 L. J. M. C.
99 ; *R.* v. *Castle View, Leicester*,
L. R. 2 Q. B. 497 ; 36 L. J. M..C.
101 ; *Lancashire JJ.* v. *Cheetham*,
L. R. 3 Q. B. 14 ; 37 L. J. M. C. 12.

[5] *R.* v. *Shepherd*, 1 Q. B. 170 ; 4
P. & D. 534.  In this category are
included reformatories established
under 17 & 18 Vict. c. 86, and 20 &
21 Vict. c. 55 : *Sheppard* v. *Bradford*,
33 L. J. M. C. 182 ; 6 C. B. N. S.
369.  But a school certified by the
Secretary of State, under 29 & 30
Vict. c. 118, as an "Industrial
School" for the reception of children
sent to it under the provisions of the
Act, by two Justices or a Magistrate,
was held rateable.  *R.* v. *West Derby
(Overseers of)*, L. R. 10 Q. B. 283 ; 44
L. J. M. C. 98, and so was a school
for training masters for paupers'
schools, though established by the
Treasury on behalf of the Lords of the
Committee of the Council of Educa-
tion : *R.* v. *Temple*, 2 E. & B. 160.

where the occupation was of the former description. In the *Mersey Dock Cases* this distinction was pointed out, and it was laid down that the latter kind of occupation only, and

restricted in the Mersey Dock Cases,

not the former, was to be exempted. It is not now therefore sufficient to entitle to exemption the occupiers of property even belonging to the Crown, to show that they use it for public purposes; but it must appear that the purposes for which the property is used are such that the occupiers may be regarded as agents on behalf of the Crown in carrying them out.

and in Greig v. The University of Edinburgh.

In *Greig* v. *The University of Edinburgh*,[1] where it was contended that the buildings of Edinburgh University were within this exemption, the effect on the law of the *Mersey Dock Cases* is stated by Lord Westbury as follows :—" On the question of exemption, anterior to the decisions of your lordships in the *Mersey Dock Case*, great looseness of expression prevailed in the language of the decisions. We had a variety of decisions in which it was held that property held for charitable purposes, being held for public purposes, was not to be regarded as liable to poor rates. The true ground of exemption was ascertained and expressed by this House in the *Mersey Dock Case*; and it was found to rest altogether upon this fact, that the poor laws did not include the Crown, the Crown not being named in the statute. The result therefore was that Crown property, and property occupied by the servants of the Crown, and (according to the theory of the Constitution) property occupied for the purposes of the administration of the Government of the country, became exempt from liability to poor rate. The confusion and looseness involved in the words ' national objects ' were thereby removed." With regard to the facts of the case before him he said, " Now nobody will contend that the functions of a

---

[1] L. R. 1 H. L. Sc. 348.

University—to teach, to instruct, to confer degrees, are functions involved in the administration of the Government of
the country. They are perfectly distinct; and it is impossible
therefore to bring the functions of a University within the
proper meaning of Government purposes ; and if so it is
impossible to hold that property granted by the Crown to
the University, or for the purposes of a University, is property
granted for the service of the Government of the country."

The rule that in order to exempt property on the ground   Present law.
of the privilege of the Crown, the occupation must be, either
that of the Crown itself, or an occupation in and for the
service of the Crown, has been firmly established by the
House of Lords,[1] and any earlier cases in which exemptions
were admitted on the ground of occupation for merely public
or national purposes must be taken to be overruled, unless
indeed their facts would bring them within the modified
form of the rule now laid down by the House of Lords.

In connection with *Greig* v. *The University of Edin-*   R. v. Shee.
*burgh, R.* v. *Shee,* and *De la Beche* v. *St. James', Westmin-*
*ster,* may be referred to. In *R.* v. *Shee,*[2] a part of the
National Gallery buildings, then occupied by the Royal
Academy, was held exempt on the ground of Crown occupation. Exemption was denied to the University of Edinburgh on the ground that the performance of the functions
of a University is no part of the duty of the Crown, and that
therefore those who perform them cannot be considered to
do so as the agents of the Crown; but it might equally well
be said that the maintenance of a Royal Academy for the
promotion of Art is not within the scope of the duty of the

---

[1] *Mersey Docks Case,* 35 L. J. M. C.
1 ; 11 H. L. C. 443 ; *Adamson* v.
*The Clyde Trustees,* 4 Macq. 931 ;
*Commissioners of Leith Harbour* v.

*Inspector of the Poor,* L. R. 1 H. L.
Sc. 17 ; and *Greig* v. *The University*
*of Edinburgh,* L. R. 1 H. L. Sc. 348.
[2] 12 L. J. M. C. 53 ; 4 Q. B. 2.

Crown, and that therefore the Royal Academy is not within the exemption. However it is not to be assumed that the Royal Academy would now, (apart from any claim to exemption under 6 & 7 Vict. c. 36, as a society for the promotion of art,) be held rateable ; as in *R.* v. *Shee*, the Court having regard to all the circumstances of the case, held that the members of the Royal Academy might " well be considered the ministers or agents of the Crown, for furthering the object for which the property of the Crown is employed."

De la Beche *v.* St. James', Westminster.

In *De la Beche* v. *St. James', Westminster*,[1] the matter in question was the rateability of the Museum of Practical Geology, which was erected upon a site belonging to the Crown, out of monies voted by Parliament, and was kept in repair by the Commissioners of Works and Public Buildings, and the current expenses of which were defrayed by the Treasury, out of monies granted to Her Majesty by Parliament for that purpose: here again it could scarcely be said that the maintenance of a Museum of Practical Geology is one of the functions of the Crown. This case is not affected by the *Mersey Dock Cases* ; that is expressly stated by Mellor, J., in *R.* v. *McCann*,[2] but whether or not it is consistent with *Greig* v. *The University of Edinburgh* is another question.

R. *v.* McCann.

In *R.* v. *McCann*[3] it was held that the exemption extended to a bridge, built by the Commissioners of Public Works and Buildings, with money borrowed from the Treasury, the tolls to be applied to the expenses of maintenance, then to the repayment of the loan for construction, and then any surplus to the consolidated fund. *R.* v. *McCann* was first decided by the Court of Queen's Bench a few months before *Greig* v. *The University of Edinburgh*, and then affirmed by the Exchequer Chamber a few days after *Greig*

---

· [1] 24 L. J. M. C. 74 ; 4 E. & B. 385.
[2] L. R. 3 Q. B. 141 ; (Ex. Ch.) 677

[1] 37 L. J. M. C. 25 ; (Ex. Ch.) 123.
[3] Ibid.

v. *The University of Edinburgh* was decided by the House of Lords, but that case was not referred to, either in argument or in the judgment of the Court.

There are three cases in which it has been held by the Court of Queen's Bench that the *Mersey Dock Cases* did not affect the exemption previously accorded to Assize Courts, &c., namely, *R.* v. *St. Martin's, Leicester*,[1] *R.* v. *Castle View, Leicester*,[2] and *Lancashire JJ.* v. *Cheetham*.[3] These three cases were all decided before *Greig* v. *The University of Edinburgh*, but do not appear to be affected by it, for the Queen is the fountain of justice to all the subjects of the realm, and buildings which are necessarily occupied for the purposes of administering justice, and for cognate objects, are within the exception as buildings really occupied for the discharge of duties arising out of the prerogatives of the Crown.[4]

There is no exemption where Crown property, a royal palace for instance, is occupied by private persons in a personal capacity for their own benefit. This was so held before the *Mersey Dock Cases*.[5]

Again, if servants of the Crown have a beneficial occupation in excess of what is necessary for performance of their service, they are rateable for the excess. See *Bute* v. *Grindall*,[6] where the ranger of a royal park was held rateable for the profits of inclosures within the park; *R.* v. *Terrott*,[7] where the commanding officer of barracks, occupying with his apartments a coach-house, stable, yard, garden, &c., was

*Marginal notes:* Recent cases on exemption of Assize Courts, &c.

No exemption where Crown property occupied by subjects for their own benefit,

or of servants of the Crown, except so far as their occupation is necessary for the duties of their service.

---

[1] L. R. 2 Q. B. 493; 36 L. J. M. C. 99.

[2] L. R. 2 Q. B. 497; 36 L. J. M. C. 101.

[3] L. R. 3 Q. B. 14; 37 L. J. M. C. 12.

[4] Per Mellor, J., in *R.* v. *Castle View, Leicester*, at p. 502.

[5] *R.* v. *Ponsonby*, 11 L. J. M. C. 65; 3 Q. B. 14; *Portland* (*Duke*) v. *St. Margaret's, Westminster*, Cald. 3 n.; *R.* v. *Chelsea Waterworks*, 2 L. J. M. C. 98; 5 B. & Ad. 156.

[6] 1 T. R. 338.

[7] 3 East, 506.

held rateable for excess; *Gambier* v. *Lydford*,[1] where the
governor of a prison was held rateable for excess consisting
of coach-house and stabling within the prison; *R.* v. *Stewart*,
*R.* v. *Edwards,* *R.* v. *Lake,* and *R.* v. *Stainsby*,[2] where it
was held that the governor of a garrison town, the com-
mander of a military district, and a storekeeper, or porter,
occupying premises belonging to the Crown, were respectively
rateable for so much of their occupation as was more than
reasonably necessary for the performance of their duties;
*Lancashire JJ.* v. *Cheetham*,[3] where, the county justices
having let the assize courts, &c., at times when they were
not required for the assizes, to the Corporation of Manchester,
who paid £600 per ann. for their use of them, the justices
were held rateable on this £600, for to that extent their
occupation was beneficial, and not merely for the purpose of
the administration of justice.

---

[1] 23 L. J. M. C. 69; 3 E. & B.
346. See *Martin* v. *West Derby
Union*, W. N., March 24th, 1883,
p. 53. In *Gambier* v. *Lydford*,
Lord Campbell, C. J., and Wightman, J. (Coleridge, J. dissenting),
held that an official residence which
would have been exempt if situate
within the prison was not exempt if
situated without the walls; but it is
submitted that if in other respects
property is entitled to the exemption,
its position is not material and does
not disentitle it    See *Congreve* v.
*Upton*, 33 L. J. M. C. 83; 4 B. & S.
857.

[2] 27 L. J. M. C. 81; 8 E. & B. 360.

[3] L. R. 3 Q. B. 14; 37 L. J. M. C.
12.

# PART III.

## HOW RATEABLE.

———

———

## RATING MUST BE EQUAL.

THE 43 Eliz. c. 2, obviously intended that rating should be equal; that is, that the contribution of each person to the support of the poor should be in proportion to the value of his property. And it appears from Sir Anthony Earby's Case,[1] in 1633, that even before that time it had been judicially declared that assessments must be equal.

But from the statute of Elizabeth, down to 1836,[2] no directions were given by statute as to the method of calculation

*The 43 Eliz. c. 2, and Sir Anthony Earby's case show that rating must be equal,*

*but no further statutory guidance on the point was given till the P. A. Act of 1836,*

———

[1] 2 Bulst. 354.
[2] When the Parochial Assessment Act was passed.

G

*though in the interval the Courts maintained the principle.*

by which equality of rating was to be arrived at. During that period, a rate if manifestly unequal, would have been quashed by the Courts;[1] and subject to such general control by the Courts, the method of arriving at equal assessments was left to the individual discretion of the respective rating authorities.

In order to rate in accordance with the principle of equality, a method of assessment is required that will affect all occupiers fairly and equally. It may be said at once—A poundage on the value of the occupation would produce the result required. But it is not so obvious how the value of the occupation is to be arrived at. It may then be said that rent affords a measure of the value of the occupation. So it might if every property were let, and let on similar terms; but different properties, intrinsically of the same value, or the same property at different times, may be occupied respectively by a yearly tenant, a lessee for a long term, or an owner. The lessee for a term ordinarily has to repair, and therefore pays less rent than the yearly tenant, and so, if the rent actually paid were taken as the value of the occupation, would pay a less rate; while an owner paying no rent, would consequently pay no rates at all; and yet in each case the value of the occupation is ex hypothesi the same, and the method of assessment employed ought to be one that would place the rate at the same amount, whether the occupier be tenant, or owner. But from the fact that rent would be a fair basis on which to calculate a poundage if only a given state of facts existed, namely if every occupation were a tenancy on similar terms, to a method of arriving at such a basis is not a far step. Assume that such a state of facts exists, or rather estimate what the rent of each particular property

*A poundage on the rent would be equal if all properties were let and let on similar terms.*

*Assume them to be so let, and calculate*

[1] *R.* v. *Audly,* 2 Salk. 526; *R.* v. *Clerkenwell,* Foley P. L. 12; 1 Const. 111; *R.* v. *Brograve,* 4 — Burr. 2491; *R.* v. *Hardy,* Cowp. 579; *R.* v. *Lakenham,* 1 Const. 116.

would be if such a state of facts did exist, and that amount the poundage<br>on the hypo-<br>thetical rent. may be taken as the basis required. Any kind of tenancy might be taken as the standard, provided that the same were taken in each case. |Previous to 1836, it had become usual This was done<br>in practice<br>before the<br>P. A. Act; in practice to take a <u>yearly tenancy as such a standard</u>, and having estimated in each case the rent a yearly tenant would pay to the landlord (the tenant paying all rates, charges, and outgoings), to rate the occupier in proportion to that amount as the value of the occupation.[1]

In 1836, this method of arriving at the value of the occu- and this was<br>the rule the<br>P. A. Act<br>enacted, pation was, with but slight modification, made uniform and compulsory by the Parochial Assessment Act,[2] which provided that rates were to be made "upon an estimate of the net annual value of the several hereditaments rated thereunto ; that is to say, of the rent at which the same might reason- ably be expected to let from year to year, free of all usual tenant's rates and taxes, and tithe commutation rent-charge, if any, and deducting therefrom the probable average annual cost of the repairs, insurance, and other expenses, if any, necessary to maintain them in a state to command such rent."

The intention of the statute is to establish a uniform rule in order to<br>promote uni-<br>formity. for assessing the value of the occupation.

It adopts as the standard of value the value of the pro- The standard<br>is the value to<br>the owner, perty to *the owner*,[3] and the value to the owner, whether he i.e., the rent<br>he would<br>receive if he occupies the property himself or lets it to a tenant, is to be measured by the amount of rent per annum it would be receive if he<br>let the pro-<br>perty on the worth to a hypothetical tenant on the terms laid down by the statute as the standard. <u>The particular terms</u>, therefore, on statutory<br>terms, which any property is in fact let, <u>are immaterial.</u> The intrinsic value of the occupation is not affected by them. If

---

[1] *R. v. Adams*, 2 L. J. M. C. 90 ;      [3] *R. v. Wells*, L. R. 2 Q. B. 542 ;
4 B. & Ad. 61.                          36 L. J. M. C. 109.
[2] 6 & 7 Will. IV. c. 96.

a particular tenant is bound· by arrangement with his landlord to bear any of the expenses which are not ordinarily incident to a yearly tenancy, that does not affect the amount
of his rateability; for it is fixed by the statute, not at the
rent he actually does pay, but at the rent a hypothetical
tenant holding on the statutory terms might reasonably be
expected to pay.[1] This is the Gross Estimated Rental or
Gross Value.

But the rent would accurately represent the value to the
owner, only if no outlay had to be incurred by him in order
to maintain the property in a state to command that rent.
The annual expense, therefore, if any, of maintaining the
property in such a state, must be deducted from the rent of
the hypothetical tenant in order to arrive at the true value
of the property to the owner.[2] After deducting these
expenses from the gross estimated rental or gross value, the
remainder is the Rateable Value.

*Marginal notes:* This is the Gross Estimated Rental or Gross Value: and deducting the outlay necessary to maintain the property in a state to command the rent, we get the Rateable Value.

## PROPERTY MUST NOT BE RATED TWICE OVER.

To rate the same property twice over would be so distinctly alien to the spirit of the 43 Eliz. c. 2, and so inconsistent with the fair and equal distribution of the burden of
supporting the poor, which it was the object of that Act to ·
effect, that this principle hardly requires to be formally
demonstrated, but a few examples of its application may be
usefully given.

*Marginal note:* Implied in the 43 Eliz. c. 2.

---

[1] *Hayward* v. *Brinkworth* (*Overseers of*), 10 L. T. N. S. 608.

[2] See *R.* v. *Wells,* L. R. 2 Q. B. 542; 36 L. J. M. C. 109; and the following cases, decided shortly before the passing of the Parochial Assess-ment Act:—*R.* v. *Adames,* 2 L. J. M. C. 90; 4 B. & Ad. 61; *R.* v. *Bridge-water Trustees,* 9 B. & C. 68; 4 M. & R. 143; *R.* v. *Tomlinson,* 9 B. & C. 162; 4 M. & R. 169.

One of the grounds of complaint in Sir Anthony Earby's Case,[1] was that the landlord was rated as well as the tenant. This, the judges of assize then held, ought not to be done, and in *Rowls* v. *Gells*,[2] Lord Mansfield said, "The landlord is never assessed for his rent, because that would be a double assessment, as his lessee had paid before."[3]

*Landlord not to be rated on rent received by him.*

So it was held that a farmer was not to be rated for his necessary stock on the farm, "for that would be in effect to make the land pay twice for one and the same thing," since the profits of the stock are included in those of the land.[4]

*Farmer not to be rated for stock,*

Upon this principle also the lord is not rateable for the quit-rents and casual profits of a manor, for they have already been rated in the hands of the occupiers.[5]

*nor lord of manor for quit-rents.*

Where a farmer was rated for his farm as a whole, and it was contended that a dairyman, his sub-tenant, was also rateable, Lord Ellenborough, C. J., said, "The principle is that the estate which has once paid shall not be made to pay again."[6] A more modern case, which may be compared with this, is *Smith & Son* v. *Lambeth*,[7] where it was sought to rate Messrs. Smith & Son for their bookstalls on the platforms of a railway station. The main question in the case was one of license or demise, but Field, J., inter alia, pointed out that the railway company were rated for the station as a whole, saying, "they" (the railway company) "are practically paying rates for the spaces upon which Messrs. Smith & Son have erected their bookstands. It is now said that Messrs. Smith & Son are also rateable. Except in the case of a joint occupation there cannot be two persons liable to be rated for the same thing."

*Tenant of part not rateable while his landlord is rated for the whole property.*

---

[1] 2 Bulst. 354.

[2] Cowp. 451.

[3] See also *R.* v. *Alberbury*, 1 East, 534.

[4] Dalton's Country Justice, edition of 1727, p. 253, c. 73.

[5] *R.* v. *Vandewall*, 2 Burr. 991; *R.* v. *Alberbury*, 1 East, at 536 arg.

[6] *R.* v. *Brown*, 8 East, 528.

[7] 9 Q. B. D. 585; 51 L. J. M. C. 106; affirmed C. A., 10 Q. B. D. 327; 52 L. J. M. C. 1.

*1882*

Only one Ry. Co. rateable in respect of through fares.

In *R.* v. *St. Pancras* (*Vestry of*),[1] it was held that where a railway company issues through tickets, for journeys to be begun on their own line and continued on the line of some other railway company, to whom they afterwards hand over a proportionate part of the fares paid to them in the first instance, the sums so handed over are not to be included for rating purposes in the receipts of the first named company, for if they were, the profits of the same line would be rated twice over, "which would be manifestly unjust."

The principle is also alluded to in *S. E. Ry. Co.* v. *Dorking*[2] and *R.* v. *Kentmere.*[3]

## REBUS SIC STANTIBUS.

Assessments to be based (*a*) on present value, and (*b*) on the assumption that the hypothetical tenant will enjoy the property in the same way as the actual occupier.

Property is to be rated 'rebus sic stantibus,' that is to say, (*a*) it must be assessed at the value it possesses at the time the assessment is made; if it increases or diminishes in value from time to time, there will be a corresponding increase or diminution in the rate, for that must be always proportioned to the then existing value, and the value of the property in the past or the future is immaterial. Moreover, (*b*) the hypothetical tenant must be assumed to use the property in the same way as the actual occupier, and to have the same facility for deriving profit from it, no more and no less. In *Staley* v. *Castleton*[4] Blackburn, J., said, "The Legislature intended that the rate should be made upon the rent which might be reasonably expected from a tenant who took the property from year to year rebus sic stantibus."

---

[1] 32 L. J. M. C. 146 ; 3 B. & S. 810.  [3] 21 L. J. M. C. 13 ; 17 Q. B. 551.
[2] 23 L. J. M. C. 84 ; 3 E. & B. 491.  [4] 33 L. J. M. C. 178; 5 B. & S. 505.

This principle is very clearly expounded and illustrated in some of the following cases.

In *Metropolitan Board of Works* v. *West Ham*,[1] Lush, J., says, "The rateable quality of land is not to be determined by what it once was, or by what it may hereafter become. If a piece of fertile land were to be covered by the ashes of a volcano, or by an inundation, it would not be rateable so long as it continued in that condition. On the other hand, in the case of a barren rock, so long as it remains a barren rock it is not rateable, but the moment it is worked as a quarry it becomes rateable. The rateable quality of land must be determined by what it was at the time the rate was made." In *R.* v. *Mast*,[2] Lord Kenyon, C. J., in deciding that an occupier who had improved his premises was to be rated on their improved value, said, "The assessment for the relief of the poor ought to be so contrived that each inhabitant should contribute in proportion to his ability, which is to be ascertained by his possessions in the parish. Every inhabitant ought to be rated according to the present value of his estate, whether it continue of the same value as when he purchased it, or whether the estate is rendered more valuable by the improvements which he has made upon it. . . . . . Suppose a person has a small piece of land in the heart of a town, which is only of small value, and he afterwards build on it, he must be rated to the poor according to its improved value with the building upon the land. In short in whatever way the owner makes his estate more valuable, he is liable to contribute to the relief of the poor in proportion to that improved estate." In *R.* v. *T. Skingle*,[3] where a farmer had been rated on the amount of his rent, which had been fixed seventeen years before, when his lease was granted, the Court

*Marginal notes:*

(a) Present, not past or future, value is the basis of rating.

A barren rock not rateable, but if quarried would become so.

Rating rises as land improves,

---

[1] L. R. 6 Q. B. 193 ; 40 L. J. M.   [2] 6 T. R. 154.
C. 55.                               [3] 7 T. R. 549.

held it to be too clear to admit of argument, that evidence was admissible to show that the farm had become of greater annual value than the rent reserved by the lease. In *R. v. St. Nicholas, Gloucester,*[1] Buller, J., said, "If a house to-day is let for £30 per annum, and to-morrow if turned into a shop would let for £50, when it is turned into a shop it shall be rated

*and falls as it depreciates in value.*

at £50."[2] So where land is turned into a railway, it ceases to be rateable at its value as land, and becomes rateable at its value as a railway,[3] whatever that may be, whether less or more than its former value as land, or if it be devoted to a purpose which renders it incapable of beneficial occupation, as in *R. v. Metropolitan Board of Works,*[4] and *Metropolitan Board of Works v. West Ham,*[5] it ceases to be rateable at all. These two cases are affirmed in *Tyne Coal Co. v. Wallsend,*[6] where Grove, J., says, "You do not rate land in respect of its value being enhanced in respect of some possible future and contingent benefit, nor do you reduce its rateability in respect of some future and contingent loss, but you take only its present value, and, as it appears to me, if any other principle were adopted it would lead to endless speculation and difficulty."

*(b) Hypothetical tenant to be assumed to use property in same way as existing occupier.*

It is laid down in *R. v. Fletton,*[7] by Cockburn, C. J., and Blackburn, J., that the true principles according to which the value of the occupation to the hypothetical tenant contemplated by the Parochial Assessment Act, is to be estimated, is to assume the continuance of those circumstances which constitute the value to the existing occupier, unless

---

[1] Cald. 262 ; 1 T. R. 723 n.

[2] See also *R.* v. *Gardner,* Cowp. 79, at 84 ; *R.* v. *Attwood,* 6 B. & C. 277, at 282 ; 5 L. J. (O. S.) M. C. 47 ; *Staley* v. *Castleton,* 33 L. J. M. C. 178 ; 5 B. & S. 505.

[3] *R.* v. *G. W. Ry. Co.* (2nd case), 21 L. J. M. C. 84 ; 15 Q. B. 379, at 395 ; *R.* v. *Manchester South Junction and Altrincham Ry. Co.*, 15 Q. B. 395 n.

[4] L. R. 4 Q. B. 15 ; 38 L. J. M. C. 24.

[5] L. R. 6 Q. B. 193 ; 40 L. J. M. C. 30.

[6] 46 L. J. M. C. 185 ; 35 L. T. N. S. 854.

[7] 30 L. J. M. C. 89 ; 3 E. & E. 450.

it be made to appear that those circumstances are about to undergo a change.

It seems to follow from this that a company or a corpora- **Restricted occupiers.** tion, or any other occupier, restricted by Act of Parliament from making the profits an ordinary tenant would make, is to be rated on the basis of the profits actually made. According however to the most recent case on the subject[1] this rule only applies where the Act has "imposed fetters" on the land itself, as distinguished from the particular occupier of it.

The following are decisions upon the question :—*R.* v. *Long-* **Cases—** *wood* (2nd case),[2] where waterworks had been constructed **R. v. Long-** by Commissioners under local Acts containing provisions the **wood (2nd case.)** effect of which was to restrict the profits. It was found by the Sessions that the annual value to the Commissioners was £490, but that the annual value to a tenant not bound by the restrictions in the Acts would be £1100. On those facts it was held that, in assessing the Commissioners, it would be wrong to assume a hypothetical tenant free from restrictions, and that the rate should be on £490—*R.* v. **R. v. Kent-** *Kentmere,*[3] where reservoirs were constructed and main- **mere.** tained by Commissioners for the purpose of affording a better supply of water to the mills and manufactories on certain streams, under a local Act authorising the Commissioners to levy rates to the amount necessary for paying the expenses of maintenance and interest on the cost of construction. It was held that the Commissioners were to be assessed at such an amount as would have been fair if the reservoirs had been a private undertaking—*Liverpool* **Liverpool** *(Mayor of)* v. *Wavertree,*[4] where a similar question arose **(Mayor of) v. Wavertree.** with regard to the Liverpool waterworks, and Blackburn, J.,

---

[1] *Chorlton-upon-Medlock (Overseers)* v. *Chorlton (Guardians)*, 51 L. J. Q. B. 458 ; 47 L. T. N. S. 96. See page 90, infra.

[2] 21 L. J. M. C. 215 ; 17 Q. B. 871.

[3] 21 L. J. M. C. 13 ; 17 Q. B. 551.

[4] 2 Ex. D. 55 n.

said, " The whole question turns on the rule given by the Parochial Assessment Act, which says the occupier is rateable at what a tenant from year to year will give as the rent, who takes the land subject to the same restrictions as those under which the appellants hold it.   Now the tenant would only give such a rent as the restrictions imposed by the statute would enable him to earn, and the rateable value is to be based upon that rent." The latter case was upheld and followed by the Court of Appeal in *Worcester* v. *Droitwich*,[1] where it was held that a Local Board, occupying waterworks and charging a low water-rate in accordance with the statute, were rateable only on the profits they actually earned, and not on the amount that might be earned by an occupier unlimited in respect of his charges.

Worcester *v.* Droitwich.

But in *Chorlton-upon-Medlock (Overseers)* v. *Chorlton (Guardians)*,[2] where a Corporation purchased and occupied baths and laundries under the provisions of various Baths and Washhouses Acts, which placed restrictions on the charges the Corporation might make for the use of the same, the Court of Queen's Bench held that the case was not governed by *Worcester* v. *Droitwich*, supra, and drew a distinction between cases where the Acts impose restrictions on the land itself and cases where the restrictions are on the particular tenant of it.   The Court held that where the latter is the case the land is to be rated at its value to an unrestricted tenant, Cave, J., saying, " If there is a restriction on the use of the tenement, the market value would of course be affected by it, but where there is simply a restriction on the use that a particular tenant may make of it, I think that it should be disregarded except in the case where the assessment is based on the amount of profit made."

Chorlton-upon-Medlock (Overseers) v. Chorlton (Guardians).

[1] 2 Ex. D. 49 ; 45 L. J. M. C. 81 ;      [2] 51 L. J. Q. B. 458 ; 47 L. T. affirmed C. A., 2 Ex. D. 58 ; 46 L. J.      N. S. 96. M. C. 241.

Although, as a rule, property is to be rated on the assumption that the hypothetical tenant would be in the same position as the party rated, and would occupy with the property in question all that is occupied with it as an entire concern by the actual tenant, there is a limitation to this rule in the case where the subject of rating is a hereditament that is capable of *a separate and beneficial occupation*. Property which fulfills that condition is not allowed to escape from rateability because it is occupied as part of a concern which in its entirety is not rateable ; either because it as a whole produces no profit, or because it falls within one of the classes of property excepted from rateability.

Although a property may for some reason be not rateable as a whole, yet if a part of it is capable of a separate beneficial occupation that part is rateable.

For instance, in *Mersey Docks and Harbour Board* v. *Birkenhead*,[1] it was held that warehouses, &c., occupied in connection with docks were rateable, because capable of separate and beneficial occupation, although the dock system as an entire concern was occupied at a loss.

Examples of rateability of a part—

(a) Where there is no beneficial occupation of the property as a whole,

The judgments of Quain, J., and Archibald, J., are very clear on the subject.

Quain, J., said, "I can find no authority to show that property of this kind is not rateable in the way in which the overseers propose to rate it, merely because the Mersey Docks and Harbour Board choose to carry on a losing concern. This is a losing concern in the hands of the present occupiers ; but they choose for some purpose or other to carry it on. That may be so, but I do not understand that that portion of the property which would let to a tenant within the meaning of the Parochial Assessment Act, is not rateable. The question is, what would a tenant give for these warehouses by the year, making the usual deductions. The case distinctly finds that there would be a rateable value for those warehouses and other matters. Therefore, it seems to me that upon that ground these items are rateable. The fact that

---

[1] L. R. 8 Q. B. 445 ; 42 L. J. M. C. 141.

they belong to a concern which as a whole is carried on by a
Dock Company at a loss is no answer to the question as to
their rateability."

Archibald, J., said : " There may be, no doubt, conceivable
cases in which the whole property may be so bound together
as to render it impossible that one part can be let without
another, and that there can be any separate letting.
There may be other conceivable cases in which the
adjuncts of the property are not lettable in any way, and
therefore, if one part of the property is not rateable
you could not rate the other. Here the fact is expressly
found that these particular properties are capable of a
separate beneficial occupation apart from their proximity to,
or connection with, the docks. I think, therefore, applying
the principle of the Parochial Assessment Act, that as each
of these items may have a separate tenant found for them, they
are separately rateable."

So in *R.* v. *Metropolitan Board of Works*,[1] a wharf and
pumping station used as part of a drainage scheme were
rated, although the sewers themselves were not rateable, because not the subject of a beneficial occupation. A distinction was attempted to be drawn in favour of the pumping
apparatus, as being a necessary adjunct to the sewers, and it
was contended that as the sewers were not rateable, this
adjunct must be exempted as being part of a non-rateable
subject. But the Court would not accede to this view. Lush,
J., said, " The machinery stands on land which is valuable
for occupation, and which would undoubtedly be rateable in
the hands of any other occupier ; and its rateable quality
cannot be affected by the particular use to which it is applied
by the board."

or (*b*) where
the concern as

An example of the rating of a part of a concern that as a

---

[1] L. R. 4 Q. B. 15 ; 38 L. J. M. C. 24.

whole was not of a rateable nature is to be found in *Guest* v. *East Dean*,[1] where surface lands with buildings, &c., occupied in connection with an iron mine, were rated at a time when iron mines themselves were not rateable. The authority of *R.* v. *Bilston* (1st case),[2] if, and so far as, at variance with the rule above laid down, is now destroyed by *Talargoch Mining Co.* v. *St. Asaph*,[3] *Guest* v. *East Dean*,[4] and *Kittow* v. *Liskeard Union*.[5] The description of property rated in *Talargoch Mining Co.* v. *St. Asaph*, was a watercourse occupied in connection with a mine, and in *Kittow* v. *Liskeard Union*, surface land with buildings, &c., occupied with a mine; neither of the mines in question being at the time subject to be rated.

a whole is not of a rateable nature.

## COMMUNIBUS ANNIS.

The principle that property is to be rated at its value 'communibus annis' is complementary to that of 'rebus sic stantibus.'

Rating Communibus annis—

Although by the principle of rebus sic stantibus property is to be rated at its present value, it must be added that present value means, not the value shown by the balance sheet of the particular year, but, the value which under present circumstances it would be worth to let *in an average year*, or taking one year with another. This is the principle of 'communibus annis.'

i.e., on value in an average year.

[1] L. R. 7 Q. B. 334; 41 L. J. M. C. 129.

[2] 5 B. & C. 851.

[3] L. R. 3 Q. B. 478; 37 L. J. M. C. 149.

[4] L. R. 7 Q. B. 334; 41 L. J. M. C. 129.

[5] L. R. 10 Q. B. 7; 44 L. J. M. C. 23.

For instance, the profits of one particular year may have been entirely swallowed up by exceptional repairs, but it by no means follows from that, that the property has no letting value. Obviously it would not be so regarded by either landlord or tenant, and corresponding observations may be made as to exceptional profits realised from some cause or other in a particular year.

*R. r. Mirfield— exceptional profits.*

A good illustration of the principle is *R.* v. *Mirfield,*[1] where one of the questions submitted to the Court was whether underwoods, which were cut down only in every twenty-first year, were liable to be rated in every year, or only in every twenty-first year, when alone profit was actually derived from them. If rated in each year the rate would naturally be based on the amount arrived at by dividing the profit of the twenty-first year by twenty-one; if rated in the twenty-first year alone, it would of course be based on the amount of profit then realised. It was held that the underwoods ought to be rated in each year, and not in the twenty-first year alone.

*R. r. Hull Dock Co.— exceptional repairs.*

In *R.* v. *Hull Dock Co.*,[2] the profits of a Dock Company, during the six months for which the rate was made, were entirely absorbed by the expenses of taking down and rebuilding a part of the Docks, but it was held that they were rateable nevertheless. Lord Ellenborough said, " The question is whether a rate can be imposed in respect of property which is generally rateable, but the profits of which, owing to certain incidental and necessary expenses, have been for a time exhausted. . . . It appears to me that this rate is well imposed, and that the average profits of the company are not liable to be merged in the partial expenditure of any particular period." Bayley, J.—" I agree that this rate is well

---

[1] 10 East, 219.   [2] 5 M. & S. 394.

imposed. The case does not state that this property communibus annis is not productive of profit, but only that
during this particular period it was not profitable. . . .
*R.* v. *Mirfield* is a clear authority that the principle
which is to govern is whether it be profitable communibus annis." Abbott, J. — " I think the company
cannot relieve themselves from this rate, by showing that,
on the occasion of some extraordinary expenditure, during the particular period for which the rate is made, that
which would have gone to the account of profits, has been
otherwise consumed." The judgment of Holroyd, J., is to
the same effect.

In *R.* v. *Agar*,[1] Lord Ellenborough said, " No doubt the   R. *v.* Agar.
fair average expenses ought to be allowed in estimating the
quantum of the rate, but not any extraordinary expenditure
which might happen to make the property unprofitable in a
particular year : for where it is the subject of annual value,
the money so laid out in one year will produce profit in the
subsequent years. . . . If valuable land in the neighbourhood
of a town be covered with buildings in one year, the expenses of that year would probably greatly exceed its profits,
but the land would not cease to be valuable and rateable on
that account."

The effect of the principle of ' communibus annis ' with
regard to repairs, is that just as in the case of the underwoods, each year is credited with, not the profits actually received in it, but the amount of profit arrived at by striking
an average between profitable and unprofitable years, so,
with regard to repairs, a deduction is to be made in each
year, not of the expense of the repairs actually done in it,
but of the probable annual cost of the repairs, &c., necessary,

---

[1] 14 East, 256.

in the words of the Parochial Assessment Act, to maintain the property in a state to command the rent.

Certain exceptions to the rule of rating on average value.

To the principle of 'communibus annis,' as stated on page 93, there is an exception in the case of certain kinds of property, such as brickfields, cemeteries and quarries, of which it is easier to give examples than a definition. The occupier of a brickfield consumes the brick earth once for all, and so is constantly diminishing the corpus of the property and its capacity to yield a profit ; so, in the case of a cemetery, the more graves sold the less remain to sell. Such properties do not, as a whole, produce a recurring annual crop of profits, but their capacity for yielding profit is limited to one crop from each portion of the whole, and the profit to the tenant in a particular year depends on how much of the crop he chooses to reap in that year.

Brickfields— where royalty paid.

In *R.* v. *Westbrook* and *R.* v. *Everest,*[1] is decided the method in which brickfields are to be rated, when, as is often the case, the occupier pays a royalty on the number of bricks actually made, in place of, or in addition to, a fixed rent.

In the first place it was contended that a brickfield ought not to be rated above the value of garden ground or agricultural land in the parish. This contention is disposed of at once by the principle of ' rebus sic stantibus,' which requires that a property which is at the time of the rate used as a brickfield, should be rated at its value as a brickfield.

Then came the question, how was that rateable value to be estimated ? Was it to vary with the number of bricks on which royalty was paid in each year, or not ? It might be argued that on the principle of ' communibus annis ' the value of the brickfield was, taking one year with another, always the same, and that the profits of a particular year were not to be regarded ; on the other hand it might be said on the

---

[1] 16 L. J. M. C. 87 ; 10 Q. B. 178.

principle of 'rebus sic stantibus' that, as it ought to be
assumed in the absence of evidence to the contrary, that the
circumstances which constitute the value to the occupier will
continue to exist unaltered, therefore the basis of the valuation should be the royalty (and other rent if any) of the past    Rated on
year. The latter method is the one to be adopted, and the         royalty (and
following example suggested in the judgment shows that it is       other rent if
                                                                  any) of the
the fairer one. Suppose two brickfields of the same size, which   preceding year.
if worked so as to be consumed in ten years by equal working
in each year, would produce £1000 per annum each, on which
suppose the rate would be £10 ; then in ten years each would
contribute £100 to the parochial authorities. But if one of
them be so vigorously worked as to be exhausted in a year, the
produce in that year will have been £10,000, and if the rate
be only £10 for that year there will have been a valuable
occupation escaping as to nine-tenths, the rate entirely ; and
in succeeding years the value may be nothing, all the brick-
earth having been worked out. But no injustice would be
done, if in every year the occupier were rated according to the
actual value in that year, and this is what the overseers must
estimate as well as they can. The amount of rent and
royalty is not conclusive of the actual value, it is only evidence on which to estimate it. For in one of these cases the
amount of the rent and royalty for the year was £159, and
the sessions had found that the rent a tenant might be expected to give without liability to royalty would be £100.
Lord Denman, C. J., said, " It may well be that, although at      When rating
the end of the year the lessee has made so many bricks that       is based on
                                                                  actual profits,
he can afford to pay £150 in royalty to his landlord, he could    allowance may
                                                                  be made for
not prudently at the beginning of the year contract at all        risk.
events to pay more than £100 ; and if so, the latter, rather than
the former, will be the sum at which the land may reasonably be expected to let from year to year ;" and the Court
accordingly held that the £100 and not the £159 was the
true basis of the rateable value.

Cemetery.

So in *R.* v. *Abney Park Cemetery Co.*,[1] where a cemetery company made profits by disposing of plots of ground for graves, and they were rated on the basis of what they actually received in the year preceding, the assessment was upheld by the Court of Queen's Bench; Blackburn, J., saying, " No injustice will be done if the Company are rated in every year according to the value which a hypothetical tenant would give for the occupation in the preceding year, and according to this rule the Company's receipts in one year will govern the rateable value of the cemetery in the next; " and Quain, J., " I think this case cannot be distinguished from *R.* v. *Westbrook.*[2] The principle of that case applies, and shows that the price of plots of ground sold in one year cannot be spread over several years for the purpose of ascertaining the rateable value."

## ENHANCED VALUE.

What meant by 'enhanced value.'

The expression 'enhanced value' is sometimes used in reference to enhancement of the value of the occupation within the parish by circumstances outside the parish, and sometimes in reference to enhancement of the value of the occupation by something which is not per se rateable, but which depends on the occupation, or of which the occupation is the 'meritorious cause.' It is enhancement in the latter sense only that is now to be discussed. Enhancement of the former description is dealt with infra, under the title of Contributive Value.

Follows from making the

Since the measure of the rateable value of a hereditament

---

[1] L. R. 8 Q. B. 515 ; 42 L. J. M. C. 124.     [2] 16 L. J. M. C. 87 ; 10 Q. B. 178.

is the rent which it might reasonably be expected to fetch, reasonable rent the measure of rateable value. and since that rent would be proportioned to the benefits the tenant would derive from the occupation, it follows that any profits which the tenant would receive in virtue of the occupation must be taken into consideration in making the assessment.

It matters not that those profits are of such a nature as to be not rateable per se. If they are due to the occupation they are to be taken into consideration in estimating the value of the occupation. The practical result of this is that Is an indirect rating of trade profits. in many cases trade profits are indirectly brought under contribution to the rates; when, that is, the occupation of something that is rateable per se is the meritorious cause of their existence, and so far as, their existence would influence the rent obtainable in the market for the occupation. Lord Denman, C. J., said, in *R.* v. *The Grand Junction Ry. Co.*,[1] "If the ability to carry on a gainful trade on land adds to the value of the land, that value cannot be excluded on the ground that it is referable to the trade," and in *R.* v. *G. W. Ry. Co.*,[2] he says that although the profits of trade carried on by the occupier of land upon it cannot be made directly the subject of the rate assessed in respect of such occupation, and the value of the occupation alone is the proper subject of rating, yet in that value is to be included whatever at the time forms part of it, whether permanently or not, and from whatever source derived, and therefore of course, not the less so although derived in any proportion from the fact of the trade being so carried on upon it. It must be borne in mind that trade profits, however directly arising out of the occupation, cannot be directly rated; the rate must be upon something which is per se

---

[1] 13 L. J. M. C. 94 ; 4 Q. B. 18.     [2] 15 L. J. M. C. 80 ; 6 Q. B. 179.

rateable, but in assessing anything that is so rateable, regard may be had to the fact that it is enhanced in value by being available for earning profits. For instance, a railway company is practically rated on profits, but it is solely in the capacity of an occupier of land that it is rateable at all.

**Different results in the case of a railway and of an ordinary tradesman.**

Now although a railway company is practically rated on its actual profits, the profits made by an ordinary tradesman, who could remove to another shop next door or in the next street and still make the same profits as before, do not affect the amount of his assessment. His profits are not due to the occupation of a particular hereditament, but the profits of a railway company are attached to the particular hereditaments they occupy.

The question whether profits are to influence an assessment, is in other words—would they influence the rent— and that depends on whether they are incident and appurtenant to the occupation,[1] or in other words on how far the particular hereditament has a monopoly of the facilities of earning them. The rent a tenant will give depends on two things;—first, What profit will he make? and second,

**Enhanced value limited in one direction by profits, and in the other by law of supply and demand.**

How many hereditaments possessing similar advantages are there in the market? In *R. v. L. & N. W. Ry. Co.*,[2] Blackburn, J., said, "In letting a thing from year to year the rent would be regulated by two matters, on the one hand, by the benefit the tenant would be likely to derive from the occupation, because he would not give more than that; on the other hand, by the nature of the property, such as its local situation, or how many persons there are who could supply him with an equally eligible thing and be willing to let it to him: for while he would not be willing to give more

---

[1] *R.* v. *Grand Junction Ry. Co.,* 13 L. J. M. C. 94; 4 Q. B. 18; *R.* v. *G. W. Ry. Co,* 15 L. J. M. C. 80; 6 Q. B. 179.

[2] L. R. 9 Q. B. 134; s. c. *R.* v. *Bedford Union,* 43 L. J. M. C. 81.

than he expected to make by it, he would not even give that
if he could get a similar thing at a lower price."[1]   The two
following cases are good illustrations.   In *R.* v. *North Ayles-*   R. *v.* North
*ford Union*,[2] the occupier of a chalk-pit, who was also a   Aylesford
Union.
cement manufacturer, realised large profits by turning the
chalk into cement at a neighbouring and separately rated
factory.   There were several other chalk-pits in the neighbourhood, the occupiers of which used the chalk for ballasting and other purposes much less profitable than cement
making.   It was held that the exceptional profits of this
particular occupier could not be taken into consideration in
rating him for the chalk-pit, because they would not influence
the rent of the hypothetical tenant, who could get equally
good chalk in the neighbourhood at a rent based on the
lower profits of ballasting.   On the other hand, in *R.* v.   R. *v.* Verrall.
*Verrall*,[3] it was held that the profits actually received by the
occupier of a race-course from the sale of tickets for the
grand stand, &c., were to be taken into consideration in
assessing him.   No reasons were given for the decision,
probably because it is obvious that in the case of a race-
course the actual profits made would be the basis of the
hypothetical tenant's rent, since they are incident to the
occupation of the particular piece of land on which the races
are held.   These two cases are not in conflict with each
other; under the circumstances existing in the former, evidence of the actual profits made would not have been relevant
to the question of what was the value of the hereditament
to let; but under the circumstances of the latter case such
evidence was relevant to that question.[4]

We have seen that the principle of enhanced value is now   Principle of
directly deducible from the statutory rule that the rent   enhanced value
before P. A.
Act.

---

[1] See *R.* v. *Tynemouth*, 12 East 46,     [4] See *Clark* v. *Fisherton Angar*,
and infra, page 103.     6 Q. B. D. 139 ; s. c. *Clark* v. *Alder-*
[2] 37 J. P. 148.     *bury Union*, 50 L. J. M. C. 33.
[3] 1 Q. B. D. 9 ; 45 L. J. M. C. 29.

which a hereditament might be reasonably expected to fetch
is the measure of its rateable value, but there are authorities
long previous to the Parochial Assessment Act,[1] which
decide that the rateable value of land is not to be limited to
its value as land, but is to include all profits arising out of, or
appurtenant to, the occupation.

Authorities on
enhanced value
previous to P.
A. Act—
R. v. Miller.

In *R.* v. *Miller*,[2] certain lands and buildings at Chelten-
ham containing a mineral spring were let for £100 per
annum, the value of the lands and buildings being only
£20 per annum, and the remaining £80 being paid for the
mineral water. The tenant was assessed for the premises,
under the description of "lands," upon the full rent of £100
per annum, and the rate was held to be good. Lord Mansfield, C. J., said, " Nothing can be plainer than the present
case. This is not a rate upon the profits of the well, but
upon *four acres of land*, let to the defendant at £100 a year,
and the value arises partly from the buildings and partly
from the spring that produces the mineral water. Therefore
the profits of the spring are *part of the produce of the
land*."

R. v. New
River Co.

*R.* v. *Miller* was followed in *R.* v. *New River Co.*,[3]
where a rate was imposed on land including a spring, as
being of the annual value of £300 ; the land alone being of
the annual value of £5. Grose, J., said, "I cannot distinguish this case from the common case of land on which corn
grows. In such case the land is assessed according to its
value, and that value is estimated according to that which it
produces : so here the land produces a spring, and the value
of it is to be computed according to the benefit which the
spring produces to the Company."

Kempe v.
Spence.

In *Kempe* v. *Spence*,[4]
De Grey, C. J., suggested that possibly an estate might
be assessed at a higher amount as having a right of

---

[1] 6 & 7 Will. IV. c. 96.    [3] 1 M. & S. 503.

[2] Cowp. 619.              [4] 2 Wm. Bl. 1244.

common annexed to it, although a right of common being
an incorporeal hereditament would not be per se rateable.
In *R.* v. *Tynemouth*,[1] Lord Ellenborough, C. J., while
deciding that a rate on tolls collected from ships passing a
certain lighthouse was bad, intimated that the tolls might
have been indirectly rated by laying a rate on the lighthouse
itself, whose light was the meritorious cause of earning the
tolls, if it were in consequence let at a larger rent. In
*R.* v. *Bradford*,[2] a canteen in barracks was demised at a
rent of £15 for the building and £510 for the privilege of
opening it as a canteen. It was held that the two sums
together, were in substance but one entire rent payable for
the occupation of a real tenement *and for the enjoyment of*
*the advantages belonging to it*, and therefore that the rateable value was to be based on the entire amount. The case
of *R.* v. *Coke*[3] does not conflict with the principle of
*R.* v. *Bradford*, because it was there considered that the
dues did not in fact arise from the occupation of the particular building, but were in virtue of a franchise or privilege
under which the proprietor of the lighthouse was at liberty
to display the light either from that or any other house.
In *R.* v. *Liverpool Exchange Co.*,[4] the proprietors of the
Liverpool Exchange, who were incorporated as a Company
by Act of Parliament, maintained a newsroom, to which, in
accordance with the Act, non-proprietors were admitted on
payment of an annual subscription. The question was whether the room was to be rated at the ordinary value of such a
room, or whether the revenue derived from the subscriptions
of non-proprietors was to be taken into account. Littledale,
J., after referring to the cases said, "These cases establish
the principle that the advantages attendant upon a building,

*R. v. Tyne-
mouth.*

*R. v. Brad-
ford.*

*R. v. Coke.*

*R. v. Liverpool
Exchange Co.*

---

[1] 12 East 46.                [3] 5 L. J. (O.S.) M. C. 8 ; 5 B. & C. 797.
[2] 4 M. & S. 317.             [4] 3 L. J. M. C. 107 ; 1 A. & E. 465.

either in respect of its situation or the mode of its occupation, are to be taken into account in estimating its rateable annual value, wherever those advantages would enable the owner of the building to let it at a higher rent than it would otherwise fetch ; but not to profits of a trade carried on in the building and not enhancing its rent," and on the ground that the revenue derived from the subscriptions was an advantage attached to the room by the Act, he held that it was to be taken into account in making the assessment.

Tied houses.

The question whether the rateable value of a brewery is to be regarded as enhanced by the fact that certain public-houses are bound to take their beer from it, has given rise to some difference of judicial opinion.

Alison *v.* Monkwear-mouth :—

In *Alison* v. *Monkwearmouth Shore*,[1] the occupier of a brewery paid a rent of £300 for the premises, £50 for the use of fixtures, and a further rent of £150 for the goodwill and trade of 33 'tied' houses. It was held by Lord Campbell, C. J., and Crompton, J., (Erle, J., dissenting), that the £150 was to be taken into account in estimating the rateable value of the brewery.

Lord Campbell, C. J., and Crompton, J.

Lord Campbell, C. J., and Crompton, J., considered that the custom of the tied houses was in fact attached by lease to the occupation of the brewery for seventeen years, and therefore was to be considered as one of the advantages incident to the occupation : and that, provided such an advantage was attached to the occupation, it was immaterial how it became so attached, whether by contract as in this case or by prescription as in the case of the soke mill referred to in argument.

Erle, J., diss.

Erle, J., on the other hand, took the view that the £150 was paid in respect of what was not a legal appurtenance to the land, but only a mere personal contract which would not, as in the case of the soke mill, pass under a demise of the land with its appurtenances.

---

[1] 23 L. J. M. C. 177 ; 4 E. & B. 13.

But in the subsequent case of *Sunderland (Overseers* Sunderland<br>(Overseers of)<br>*v.* Sunderland<br>Union.
*of*) v. *Sunderland Union*[1] it was held by Erle, C. J., and
Smith, J. (Byles, J., dissenting), that the rateable value
of public houses that were obliged by contract to take their
beer from a particular brewery, and which paid a less rent in
consequence, was not thereby decreased nor that of the
brewery increased.

Erle, C. J., and Smith, J., rested their decision on the Erle, C. J.,<br>and Smith, J.
ground that although a tied public-house pays less money
rent than a free house, that is because it pays part of the
rent in the shape of the landlord's profit on the beer he sells,
and the value of the occupation cannot be altered by the
method of paying the rent.

Byles, J., in dissenting from the judgment of the majority Byles, J., diss.
of the Court, said that part of the value of a tied house is
transferred to the brewery just as part of the value of some
of the ornamental squares in the metropolis is by private
contracts, under which they must for a long term of years
be used only as squares, transferred to the surrounding
houses, and there included in the increased rateable value
which the ornamental square confers on the houses that
surround it.

There seems to be a conflict between these two cases. It Conflict of<br>cases.
is not for us to say which view is the more correct one, but
for a fuller statement of the arguments on either side the
reader is referred to the reports. One judge dissented from
the judgment of the Court in each case.

But besides Enhancement of the value of the occupation Enhancement<br>by fixtures.
by Trade Profits there is what may be called Enhancement
by Fixtures. If the owner of a manufactory, for instance,
annexes to the freehold, machinery which adapts it for the

---

[1] 34 L. J. M. C. 121 ; 18 C. B. N. S. 531.

carrying on of a particular industry, and demises it in that condition, it is obvious that the value of the occupation to a tenant is something over and above the value of a building of four bare walls. On the other hand it is also obvious that mere movable office furniture which each tenant puts in when he comes, and takes away or sells to his successor, when he leaves, cannot be regarded as an enhancement of the value of the occupation. But between these two extremes there is an intermediate class of articles, which though not annexed to the freehold so as to form part of it, yet are to some extent attached to it, and which would in practice be commonly let with the building. It is sometimes a nice question whether articles of this intermediate description are to be regarded as an enhancement of the value of the occupation or not, and when as frequently happens; for instance in the case of a railway or gas company, there never has been a letting, because the same persons are both owners and occupiers, there is a need of some recognised principle· on which to determine whether such articles are to be taken into consideration or not in making the assessment. We recur in the first place to the rule that the rent of a hypothetical tenant is the measure of value, and we ask with regard to any particular article, whether the use of it would be one of the advantages conferred on the tenant in return for that rent ? Would the article be let with the hereditament on a demise to a yearly tenant ? We are assisted in answering that question by considering whether it is essential to the carrying on of the particular business for which the heredi- tament is intended; and when we find that the article or machine is to some extent attached to, though not so far as to render it part of, the freehold, we test the nature of the attachment by inquiring whether it was intended at the time of the attachment that the article should permanently remain attached to the building, and whether the attachment was made with a view to the improvement of the building, or

Articles intermediate between office furniture on the one hand, and machinery annexed to the freehold on the other.

Whether essential to the business.

Whether intended to remain permanently attached for improvement of the building, or merely for more convenient use as a chattel.

merely for the more convenient use of the article as a chattel.

The cases on the subject are very consistent in the general Cases. rules they establish, if not so uniform in their application to particular articles.

The first case bearing on the subject is *R. v. St. Nicholas,* R. v. St. *Gloucester.*[1]  The Corporation of Gloucester had erected a Nicholas, Gloucester. weighing machine in the street by the side of a house, so that part of the machine was within the house, and they were rated as occupiers of a "machine-house." The question was whether the assessment was to be made on the value of the house independently of the weighing machine, or whether the house was to be regarded as enhanced in value by the profits derived from the weighing of waggons, &c. It was held that those profits were to be taken into consideration in making the assessment, on the ground that the machine was in fact annexed to the freehold, and that the machine and house were one entire thing.

In *R. v. Hogg,*[2] the question was whether a building called R. v. Hogg. "The Engine House" was to be rated at the mere value of the building or as enhanced in value by the machine within it. It was held that the rating was to be on the enhanced value on the ground that the case was governed by *R. v. St. Nicholas, Gloucester,* and also on two other grounds (not material to the present subject of discussion), namely—that the house and engine were in fact let together as one entire subject; (which cannot be regarded as by itself a conclusive reason, or as more than evidence as to whether they would be let together to the hypothetical tenant ;)—and that personal property was rateable by law and ought to be rated where practicable ; a reason which has lost its force since the exemption of personal property from rateability.

---

[1] Cald. 262 ; 1 T. R. 723 n.        [2] Cald. 266 ; 1 T. R. 721.

R. *v.* Leith.

In *R.* v. *Leith*,[1] the question (under a local Act containing the words "tenements, hereditaments, or premises") was whether a landing place was to be regarded as enhanced in value by a floating pier made fast to the wall of the building on the shore. It was held that it was, on the ground that it would be difficult to say the pier was not part of the premises, and even if it were not it was an accessory to them.

R. *v.* Morrison.

But in *R.* v. *Morrison*,[2] it was held that a shipbuilding-yard was not to be regarded as enhanced in value by a floating dock, which was moored opposite the yard when a vessel was cradled in it for the purpose of being repaired. This case was distinguished from *R.* v. *Leith* on the ground that the dock was not permanently fixed to the yard. Lord Campbell, C. J., said it had no necessary connection with the yard, and the two might easily be separately occupied; which distinguishes it from the cases of the machine-house and the engine-house, *R.* v. *St. Nicholas, Gloucester*[3] and *R.* v. *Hogg*.[4]

R. *v.* Birmingham and Staffordshire Gas Co.

In *R.* v. *Birmingham and Staffordshire Gas Co.*,[5] Lord Denman, C. J., says it is of itself sufficient to invalidate the rate, that houses to which machinery is attached are not rated according to the increased value arising from the machinery, and that "even where the machine has not been attached, a house has been held rateable in respect of it, if the value of the house was increased by the machine;" that is to say, since value must mean value to let, if the use of the machine is one of the advantages to be enjoyed by the tenant in virtue of the occupation.

R. *v.* Guest.

In *R.* v. *Guest*,[6] Lord Denman, C. J., lays down the rule as follows :—"That real property ought to be rated according to its actual value, as combined with the machinery attached

---

[1] 21 L. J. M. C. 119 ; 1 E. & B. 121.     [4] Cald. 266 ; 1 T. R. 721.
[2] 22 L. J. M. C. 14 ; 1 E. & B. 150.     [5] 6 L. J. M. C. 92 ; 6 A. & E. 634.
[3] Cald. 262 ; 1 T. R. 723 n.     [6] 7 L. J. M. C. 38 ; 7 A. & E. 951.

to it, without considering whether the machinery be real or
personal property so as to be liable to distress or seizure
under a fieri facias or whether it would descend to the heir
or executor, or belong at the expiration of a lease to landlord
or tenant."

The rule as here laid down clearly applies the doctrine of
enhancement to machinery not so attached as to be part of
the freehold.

In *R.* v. *Southampton Dock Co.,*[1] the Sessions had found
as a fact that certain cranes, steam engines, and other like
ponderous machinery in the Southampton Docks, although
attached to the freehold, were capable of being detached
from it as easily and with as little injury to it, as other
fixtures put up for the purposes of the trade of the tenant
and usually valued as between incoming and outgoing
tenant, and it was contended that they ought to be treated
as stock in trade and not as an enhancement of the value
of the occupation. "But," said Lord Campbell, C. J., in
delivering the considered judgment of the Court, "this is a
rate upon buildings to which machinery is attached for the
purposes of trade;" and, following and affirming *R.* v. *Birmingham and Staffordshire Gas Co.*[2] and *R.* v. *Guest,*[3] he
held that the machinery was not to be placed under the
head of stock in trade and tenant's capital, but was to be
taken into account in rating the realty.

In *R.* v. *North Staffordshire Ry. Co.,*[4] a similar question
was raised with regard to machinery, &c., belonging to
a railway company, and Cockburn, C. J., in delivering the
judgment of the Court, said, "The articles to which such
a question may have reference may be divided into three
classes—first, things movable, such as office and station

*R. v. South-
ampton Dock
Co.*

*R. v. North
Staffordshire
Ry. Co.*

---

[1] 20 L. J. M. C. 155; 14 Q. B.
587.
[2] 6 L. J. M. C. 92; 6 A. & E. 634.
[3] 7 L. J. M. C. 38; 7 A. & E. 951.
[4] 30 L. J. M. C. 68; 3 E. & E.
392.

furniture ; secondly, things so attached to the freehold as to become part of it; and thirdly, things which though capable of being removed, are yet so far attached as that it is intended that they shall remain permanently connected with the railway or the premises used with it, and remain permanent appendages to it as essential to its working. It is clear, that in respect of the first class of articles a deduction should be allowed. It is equally clear that no deduction should be allowed as to the second. As to the third, the question is finally settled by the decision of this Court in the case of *The Queen* v. *The Southampton Dock Co.*"[1]

R. v. Lee :—  In *R.* v. *Lee*,[2] a similar question was raised with regard to the plant of a gas company. The exhaustive judgments of Cockburn, C. J., Blackburn, J., and Lush, J., re-affirmed *R.* v. *Southampton Docks* and *R.* v. *North Staffordshire Rl. Co.* and further elucidated the subject. Cockburn, C. J., after referring to *Walmsley* v. *Milne*,[3] said, " So here, we cannot doubt that when these purifiers, and gas-holders, and the steam engine and boiler, which are absolutely essential to the working of the manufactory, were erected, it was intended that they should remain where they were for the benefit of the inheritance. I therefore think, that upon both the grounds which I have specified, the articles in question are so connected with the freehold as to show an *intention that they should remain permanently attached,* and that the Sessions were wrong in allowing deductions in respect of them."

Blackburn, J.  Blackburn, J.:—"The rule laid down has been, that where things are attached to the premises so as to become part of them, although there may be a right to remove them they are to be looked upon as part of the premises. But if

Cockburn,
C. J.

---

[1] 20 L. J. M. C. 155 ; 14 Q. B. 587.    [3] 29 L. J. C. P. 97 ; 7 C. B. N. S.
[2] L. R. 1 Q. B. 241 ; 35 L. J.    115.
M. C. 105.

anything is fastened to the premises so as still to remain a chattel, though fixed and steadied for the purposes of use, it never ceases, to use the phrase in the case of *Hellawell* v. *Eastwood*,[1] to have the character of a movable chattel, though fixed for the purpose of having the enjoyment of it. The ordinary illustration is the case of a mirror, which is screwed to the wall, but still remains a movable chattel, and is no part of the premises. On the other hand a grate which is built into a chimney, although it is capable of being removed, would still be fixed to the premises, so as to be part of them, and therefore part of what would be considered as let to the hypothetical tenant and for which he would pay rent. In *Hellawell* v. *Eastwood*,[1] the Court were dealing with machinery which was fixed, screwed, and attached to the premises, and they laid down the rule as being a matter of fact depending upon the circumstances in each case, but principally upon two considerations, first, the mode of annexation to the soil or fabric of the house, and the extent to which it is united to them, whether it can be easily removed, integre, salve et commode, or not without injury to itself or the fabric of the building; secondly, and this is worthy of attention, on the object and purposes of the annexation, whether it was for the permanent and substantial improvement of the dwelling; in the language of the Civil Law 'perpetui usus causâ,' or in that of the Year Book 'pour un profit del inheritance,' or merely for temporary purposes or the more complete enjoyment and use of it as a chattel. In the case before them the Court thought that the articles in question were only put up, and fastened for the temporary use and enjoyment of them as chattels; but they clearly and distinctly pointed out two important elements for consideration : first, *the degree of annexation;*

Tests—the mode and the object of the annexation.

---

[1] 20 L. J. Ex. 154 ; 6 Exch. 295.

and secondly, *the object of the annexation.— Was the article attached for the improvement of the inheritance or for the enjoyment only of the article itself?*"

*Lush, J.*

Lush, J. :—"I apprehend that the premises to be rated are to be taken as they are, with all the fittings and appliances by which the owner has adapted them to a particular use, and which would pass as part of the premises if they were demised to a tenant. That seems to me to express what is laid down in the two cases which have been referred to. Wherever such fittings and appliances have become so far a part of the premises as to pass by a demise of the premises, they form a part of the rateable subject of the inheritance for the purpose of rating. When we have to apply this test to any particular state of circumstances, the question is not what a tenant might remove, not what might be taken in execution under a writ against the owner, but what, *as between the landlord and tenant, would pass as part of the premises.*"

*R. v. Halstead.*

*R. v. Halstead* [1] in which the question was whether certain machinery in a silk factory was to be taken into account in rating it, further illustrates the principles laid down in the preceding case. Cockburn, C. J., said, " According to the recent cases, if the chattels are so fixed to the freehold that on a demise they would pass with the premises, then they may be taken as part of the rateable value. But here the Sessions find they are not so attached to the freehold, but are merely fixed with a view to steady them. Therefore the finding concludes the case. Blackburn, J., said that the machines, &c., " may be severable by the sheriff or by any one else, but so long as they are attached to the building so as to be part of the premises, they would be liable to be taken into account. But in saying they are attached, we

---

[1] 32 J. P. 118.

must look to the character in which they are so attached, whether it is in the sense of being accessions to the fixed property, or merely attached in the sense of steadying the machines while using them. Thus it plainly appears from the case that they are fixed merely to steady them and in no other sense, and therefore I think they form no part of the rateable value.

In *Chidley* v. *West Ham*,[1] where the question was raised with regard to the machinery and fixtures of a distillery, Blackburn, J. said, "Whatever is fixed to the realty so as to pass as landlord's fixtures in a demise of the premises, must be taken to be part of the premises for the purpose of ascertaining its rateable value. The question of what kind of fixtures comes under this description is treated at length in *Holland* v. *Hodgson*.[2]"

*Chidley v. West Ham.*

Lastly, in *Laing* v. *Bishopwearmouth*,[3] where the machinery in question was that of a ship-building yard, Cockburn, C. J., after saying that the law was settled by the above-mentioned cases, went on to say, "Applying the rule established by these decisions to the present case, it appears to us, after having carefully considered the character of the machinery in question, that the whole of it, though some of it may be capable of being removed without injury to itself or the freehold, *is essentially necessary to the ship-building business* to which the appellant's premises are devoted, *and must be taken to be intended to remain permanently attached to them so long as those premises are applied to their present purpose.*"

*Laing v. Bishopwearmouth.*

Throughout the cases there is an entire uniformity of principles. For details as to the particular items brought before the Court, reference must be made to the cases themselves.[4]

---

[1] 32 L. T. N. S. 486 ; 39 J. P. 310.
[2] L. R. 7. C. P. 328 ; 41 L. J. C. P. 146.
[3] 3 Q. B. D. 299 ; 47 L. J. M. C. 41.
[4] Other cases bearing on the

I

## THE PAROCHIAL PRINCIPLE.

**The parish the unit of area.**

The 43 Eliz. c. 2, constituted the parish the unit of area for the operation of the Act.

It provided that the churchwardens and overseers of each parish should raise the money required for the relief of the poor by taxation of the inhabitants and occupiers of rateable property within the parish.

**When part only of a property is within a particular parish—how to be rated.**

One consequence of the parish being the unit of area is that where rateable property extends into more than one parish, each of the parishes into which the property extends must rate the portion within it and that portion only. The Parochial Assessment Act prescribes that each rateable hereditament is to be assessed at its net annual value. The portion of a property that is within a particular parish is for rating purposes a separate hereditament; the Parochial Assessment Act requires it to be assessed at its net annual value, and its net annual value will be based on its net profits.

**Parochial principle,**

The parochial principle requires then that the portion of a property within a particular parish should be rated in proportion to the net profits earned by that portion of the property. The Parochial Assessment Act, now that it exists, is a convenient step in the argument, but that Act did not create any new principle, it merely declared what was already involved in the 43 Eliz. c. 2, and it was recognised before the Parochial Assessment Act was passed[1] that the parochial

**deducible from the 43 Eliz. c. 2.**

subject are *R.* v. *Granville* (*Lord*) 9 B. & C. 188 ; *R.* v. *Haslam*, 17 Q. B. 220 ; *Haley* v. *Hammersley*, 30 L. J. Ch. 771 ; 3 De Gex, F. & J. 587 ; *Staley* v. *Castleton*, 33 L. J. M. C. 178 ; 5 B. & S. 505. See also Chitty's Statutes, 4th ed., Vol. V., sub. tit. Poor-notes to 43 Eliz. c. 2, pages 238, 239.

[1] *R.* v. *Kingswinford*, 7 B. & C. 236 ; s. c. *R.* v. *Dudley Canal Co.*, 6 L. J. (O. S.) M. C. 3 ; *R.* v. *Lower Mitton*, 8 L. J. (O. S.) M. C. 57 ; 9 B. & C. 810 ; *R.* v. *Oxford Canal Co.*, 10 B. & C. 163 ; 5 M. & R. 100.

principle as above laid down was one of the necessary developments of the parochial principle in its simplest form, namely, that the parish is the unit of area. Bayley, J. says in *R.* v. *Lower Mitton*:[1] "It is now fully established that the proprietors of a canal or navigation are rateable as occupiers of the land covered with water in the particular parish in which the canal lies, *and it follows from thence*, and it was so decided in *R.* v. *Kingswinford*,[2] that they are rateable in each parish in proportion to the profit which that part of the land covered with water which lies in the parish produces."

Now where a property extends into different parishes it would be a very convenient way of arriving at the rateable value of the part in a particular parish, to first ascertain the net profits of the whole, and then to apportion to the part in the parish in question a share of those net profits in the ratio of the length or area of that part to the length or area of the whole, and to base the rateable value on the amount of net profits so apportioned. In the case of railways, canals, and such undertakings, this method would avoid many intricate calculations, and it was at one time contended that the rateable value of the part of the line in the parish should be ascertained by this method, which is called the mileage system. But unless it were the case that the receipts and outgoings were respectively uniform in amount on every mile of the line, or that all the receipts were for the use of the line as a whole and all the expenses were incurred with respect to the line as a whole, the result arrived at by the mileage system would not represent correctly the net profits of the part of the line within the parish in question, and consequently not the rateable value. In practice the net profits do vary in different places, but under the mileage system a mile

*Mileage system,*

*not allowable.*

---

[1] 8 L. J. (O. S.) M. C. 57 ; 9 B. & C. 810.

[2] 7 B. & C. 236 ; s. c. *R.* v. *Dudley Canal Co.*, 6 L. J. (O. S.) M. C. 3.

of line in a part of the system where the profits actually earned are greatest, would be assessed at the same amount as a mile in some other part where the profits actually earned are least, although the net annual value of the former would not be the same as that of the latter. This would not be in accordance with the parochial principle which requires the rateable value to be based on the actual profits of the part in question, and the Courts have refused to recognise the mileage system.

In *R.* v. *Kingswinford*,[1] where one-twelfth portion of a canal was within the parish in question, it was contended that that portion should be rated on one-twelfth of the net profits of the whole canal ; but the Court held that it was to be rated on the actual amount of profits made upon it, and not on a part of the whole amount earned along the whole line of the canal in proportion to the length of the part of the canal in the parish. Bayley, J. said, "I am of opinion that the Company ought to be rated in each particular parish in proportion to the profit which they derive from the land there used by them for the purpose of the canal. If a canal runs through six different parishes, and there is the same traffic through the whole line of the canal, every part of the canal will earn an equal proportion of the tolls. But it may happen that in that part of the canal situate in one parish there may be double or treble the traffic which there is in any other of the six. Why are the other parishes to have any part of the tolls earned in that parish ? The land in those parishes contributes nothing towards earning the sum derived in the other parish from the use of the land there. The true principle is this : a canal company is to contribute to the relief of the poor in each parish through which the canal passes in proportion to the profit which they derive

---

[1] 7 B. & C. 236 ; s. c. *R.* v. *Dudley Canal Co.*, 6 L. J. (O. S.) M. C. 3.

from the use of their land in that parish. If the profit
arising from a given quantity of land vary in different parishes,
the rate must vary in the same proportion." Again, in *R.* v.       R. v. Oxford
*The Oxford Canal Co.*,[1] Bayley, J. says: "The Company are         Canal Co.
rateable in each parish for the net annual profit of the
portion of the canal lying in that parish; in other words,
for what the canal in each parish earns." It has also been
held that it is not permissible in rating a Water Company to       Chelsea water-
divide the rateable value of the whole among the different        works Co. *v.*
parishes according to the quantity of land occupied by the        Putney.
apparatus in each parish.[2]

It was however attempted as railways became developed,
with their necessarily intricate accounts, to obtain a recognition of the mileage system as a legitimate one in their
case. It was urged that the mileage system was a simple
and convenient one, while the parochial principle was so
inapplicable to the circumstances of railways that it was
scarcely practicable to act upon it; but it was finally decided    Finally decided
by the judgment of the Court in the three cases of *R.* v.          that parochial
*The London, Brighton, and South Coast Ry. Co.*;[3] *R.* v.         principle must
*The South Eastern Ry. Co.*;[3] and *R.* v. *The Midland Ry.*       not be de-
*Co.*,[3] that the parochial principle must in no case be de-       parted from.
parted from.

The mileage system of calculation may however be ap-           When use may
plied where the profits are uniform on every part of the           be made of the
line,[4] or in the apportionment of expenses (such as those       mileage
of 'central superintendence'), which, though arising locally,      system.
are incurred in respect of the line as a whole.[5] For in
such cases as these the results of the mileage system and the

---

[1] 10 B. & C. 163 ; 5 M. & R. 100.          [4] *R.* v. *Woking*, 5 L. J. M. C. 17 ;
[2] *Chelsea Waterworks Co.* v. *Putney*,      4 A. & E. 40.
29 L. J. M. C. 236 ; s. c. *R.* v. *Putney*      [5] *R.* v. *Great Western Railway Co.*
(*Overseers of*), 3 E. & E. 108.            (2nd case), 21 L. J. M. C. 84 ; 15 Q.
[3] 20 L. J. M. C. 124 ; 15 Q. B. 313.       B. 379, 1085.

parochial principle coincide, and therefore there is no departure from the latter, in the use of the former for convenience of calculation. Wherever the result of each method would be the same, either may be employed; where the results would be different, the parochial principle must be followed.

Actual receipts and expenses within the parish.

To arrive at the net profits of the part of a property that is within the parish we must ascertain first its gross receipts and then its expenses. Its gross receipts may consist either of payments wholly earned within the parish, or of a share of payments that are earned partly within and partly without the parish, or may be made up of items belonging to each of these classes. The apportionment necessary to calculate the items falling under the second head may be effected in any method which will be accurate. The items of which the expenses consist, will fall under corresponding heads, and with regard to both expenses and receipts, what has to be ascertained is the amount actually due to the part of the property that is within the parish in question.

Immaterial where profits received.

It is not material whether the profits are received within or without the parish,[1] the important point is whether they are produced by the land within the parish.[2]

Question of contributive value.

That the rateable value of the part of the property within the parish must be proportioned to its actual profits instead of to its length or area, or in other words that the parochial principle must prevail over the mileage system, is clearly established, but there has arisen a difficult question as to what are to be included in the profits of the land. Are they to be limited to the profits earned on it, or are they to include any share of profits which it enables the land in another parish to earn? This will be treated under the head of Contributive Value.

---

[1] *R.* v. *New River Co.*, 1 M. & S. 503; *R.* v. *Barnes*, 1 B. & Ad. 113.    [2] *R.* v. *Lower Mitton*, 8 L. J. (O. S.) M. C. 57; 9 B. & C. 810.

## CONTRIBUTIVE VALUE.

The question of <u>Contributive Value</u> is mainly of interest Contributive<br>value. in connection with the Rating of Railways, though there is nothing to confine its applicability to them, to the exclusion of other kinds of property extending like them over different parishes.

Apart from the profits,·if any, which are earned upon a Illustration of. branch line, or an outlying portion of a railway, it may be of value as a feeder to the main line, because contributing to the profits of the main line by bringing traffic upon it. It not unfrequently happens that such branch lines are worked by the occupier of the main line when their intrinsic value as measured by the earnings upon them is nothing, or even though there is a loss upon them.

In rating a branch line in a particular parish, is this fact What the<br>question is. that it is valuable as a feeder to a line in some other parish to be taken into consideration in estimating its rateable value, or are the profits it produces in the first mentioned parish alone to be considered in assessing it there ? That is the question of contributive value.

It will not be possible, for two reasons, to give to this question an answer which will apply to all cases, or indeed to definitively answer it at all. In the first place the answer will depend in each case on the particular facts therein ; and in the second, the judicial decisions do not all appear consistent with one another. Briefly speaking, it is said on the Its uncertain<br>state. one hand, that the value as feeder is part of the fruits of the occupation in the parish where the branch exists, and therefore is an element of the rateable value there, and on the other that the parochial principle as applied to railways involves estimating the value of the part of a railway in a particular parish, by taking into consideration the receipts and expenses within the parish alone. Sometimes the one and sometimes the other of these views has formed the ratio decidendi.

**Difficulty of applying the P. A. Act to properties extending over different parishes.**

The question of contributive value is an example of the difficult problems that present themselves for solution in the course of applying the rule of the Parochial Assessment Act[1] to properties of a very different nature from those that were in the contemplation of the Legislature when that rule was laid down. Indeed, so serious were those difficulties regarded when they first arose, that Lord Campbell, C. J., in one case[2] postponed judgment in the hope that the Legislature would relieve the judges from the task of solving them, by interposing to lay down rules more easily applicable to the rating of railways. But no such interposition took place, and the details of railway rating had to be developed out of first principles.

**Preliminary points.**

There are three points to which attention may be called in the first place by way of clearing the ground.

**(1) Objection on ground of double rating.**

(1) It was said by Erle, J., in *S. E. Ry. Co.* v. *Dorking*,[3] that if the branch line were rated for contributive value, there would be a double rating in respect of the same profits, since the parishes on the main line in which the profits of the traffic contributed by the branch are actually received would be entitled to rate the main line on them as profits made in the parish. It is assumed by Erle, J., that no deduction, on the ground that some of these profits belong to the branch, could be made in the parishes on the main line, and this view seems to derive support from some dicta of Lord Denman, C. J., in *R.* v. *L. & S. W. Ry. Co.*,[4] where he says, "the subject matter of rate in each particular parish is, no doubt, the beneficial occupation of the land there, and

---

[1] 6 & 7 Will. IV. c. 96.
[2] *R.* v. *Great Western Railway Co.* (2nd case), 21 L. J. M. C. 84 ; 15 Q. B. 379, 1085.
[3] 23 L. J. M. C. 84 ; 3 E. & B. 491 ; infra, page 125.
[4] 11 L. J. M. C. 93 ; 1 Q. B. 558.

you cannot draw into the rate the value of the occupation of buildings elsewhere; yet as you are about to rate on the value in the parish however occasioned, you cannot strike off any portion, because it would not have existed but for the occupation of buildings in another parish; still it exists, and in the parish, and therefore cannot escape the rate there. Suppose A. B. occupying an entire tenement, as an inn, in two parishes, C. and D.; the lodging part of the building in C., and the tap and stables in D. There would be two rates, but could the owner say in C., 'True it is that which I occupy here is de facto more valuable than a mere dwelling or boarding-house, but that is in a great measure because it is connected with the tap and stables in D.; you must reject what is referable to that connection, and rate me here as if I occupied an inn without a tap or stables; you must suppose a demise only of the parts in C. and rate on the rent to be given only for what that demise would pass to me.'" On the other hand, Lord Campbell, C. J., said, in *S. E. Ry. Co.* v. *Dorking,* that if 'the appellants were rated in a parish on the branch line in respect of the value of the branch line as a feeder, then "in estimating the profits in the parishes through which the main line passes, there ought to be a deduction in respect of what is paid for the line which is worked as a feeder to the main line." It is submitted that if the rateable value of the branch line be enhanced by its value as a feeder, then the profits when received on the main line ought to be, and could be, subjected to the deduction of an equivalent amount, to be regarded as one of the expenses of earning them.

If that is so, then Contributive Value is a question which concerns the parishes alone and not the railway companies, for to the latter it is immaterial which way it is settled, since if their rateable value is increased by it in one parish it will be correspondingly diminished in another.

C. V. a question between parishes.

(2) Another objection to Rating on Contributive Value

(2) Objection on ground of

difficulty of calculation.

is pointed out by Erle and Crompton, JJ., and Lord Campbell, C. J., in *S. E. Ry. Co.* v. *Dorking,* and by Shee, J., in *The Haughley Case,* namely, the difficulty of measuring it, and distinguishing what is to be credited to the branch from the general profits of the occupation on the main line. Still the difficulties there may be in carrying it out cannot affect the question of whether it is right or not in principle. If it is, then those difficulties must be faced like others.

(3) Branch when incorporated with trunk to be treated as the same concern.

(3) A third point which it will be of assistance to bear in mind, is that where a branch is incorporated with a main line, is worked, that is, as part of the same concern, then, subject to possible exceptions where the fusion is not complete, the two are to be considered as one property for the purpose of estimating rateable value; for the hypothetical tenant must be assumed to be tenant of both, since the object of assuming his existence at all is to ascertain what a tenant would give " by way of rent from year to year in order to be placed as occupier *in the same position as the party rated.*" [1] or in other words, the supposition of a tenancy " is only a mode of ascertaining the existing value of the occupation to the *existing occupier.*" [2] A direct authority that where a branch is absorbed into the trunk they are to be treated as one for the purpose of rating calculations is *R.* v. *G. W. Ry. Co.* (2nd case).[3]

Circumstances in which the question of C. V. arises.

To determine whether the occupier of a branch line is to be rated for its value as a feeder, we must first see that he profits by it, and secondly that he does so as part of the fruits of his occupation. If a branch contributes traffic to a main line which is in the hands of another and independent occu-

---

[1] Per Lord Denman, C. J. in *R.* v. *G. W. Ry. Co.* (1st case), 15 L. J. M. C. 80; 6 Q. B. 179.

[2] Per Lord Denman, C. J. in *R.* v.

*Grand Junction Ry. Co.,* 13 L. J. M. C. 94; 4 Q. B. 18.

[3] 21 L. J. M. C. 84; 15 Q. B. 379, 1085.

pier, then (in the absence of any agreement between the respective occupiers, such for instance as existed in the *New-market Case*, infra, page 124), it is clear that there is no enhancement of the value of the occupation of the branch on the score of contributive value : it passes into the hands of strangers, and the occupier of the branch has no control over it, and gets no profit out of it. But if the occupier of a main line constructs, or buys, or takes a lease of, a branch which contributes traffic to the main line, and occupies the branch himself, then the occupier of the line which has a feeder value is also the person who profits by that feeder value. The same is the case where the portion of line under consideration is what would be ordinarily called, not a branch, but, a portion of the main line, and indeed it makes no difference which we call it, since as we have seen all the lines worked as parts of the same system are to be treated as one concern in estimating rateable value ;[1] but it will be convenient to speak of the part of line which contributes the traffic, as the branch, and the part where the profits are actually received, as the main line. Then there is the less common, but possible, case where the occupier of the branch, though not in occupation of the main line also, yet contrives as in the *Newmarket Case*, infra, page 124, to put something into his own pocket by reason of the value of the branch as a feeder to the main line.

It will now be convenient to briefly summarise the chief Cases. cases so far as they bear on the principle of Contributive Value, but omitting any reference to the three points already touched upon on pages 120-122, and we can then, treating these cases as a whole, endeavour to ascertain their result. This plan will perhaps be preferable to taking them one by one and quoting from the judgments in each, as some of the

---

[1] *R.* v. *Great Western Railway Co.* (2nd case), 21 L. J. M. C. 84 ; 15 Q. B. 379, 1085.

judgments are of considerable length, and short quotations might be misleading, especially as the effect of the ipsissima verba depends to some extent on the state of facts before the Court in each particular case.

**Newmarket case.**
(1) *The Newmarket Ry. Co.* v. *St. Andrew the Less, Cambridge.*[1] (Jan. 1854.)

**Facts.**
The B. Co.—in pursuance of an agreement, that if the A. Co. would construct and work a certain branch line, the B. Co. would in consideration of its value to them as a feeder to their line, pay to the A. Co., whenever they did not earn **Guarantee.** enough to pay a dividend of 3 per cent., such sum as would enable them to make up their dividend to that rate—had paid in one year a sum of £3705 to the A. Co.

**Held not rateable on sum paid under guarantee.**
Held, by Coleridge and Erle, JJ. (diss. Lord Campbell, C. J.), that, in assessing the branch line of the A. Co., the £3705 paid by the B. Co. was not to be taken into consideration, but only the profits actually earned upon the branch line.

**Summary of judgments— Erle, J.**
Erle, J.—The hypothetical tenant would not get the benefit of the sum paid under the guarantee :

the rate upon that sum would not be legal, because it would really fall not upon the occupier but on the guarantor : and,

that sum is not a profit made in the parish, and is not affected by the principle that the respective value of rateable subjects in different parishes may be increased by their combined operation.

**Coleridge, J.**
Coleridge, J.—That sum is not part of the fruits of the occupation, and the hypothetical tenant would not necessarily get it.

---

[1] 23 L. J. M. C. 76 ; 3 E. & B. 94 ; cf. *R.* v. *Lapley*, 9 B. & S. 568.

Lord Campbell, C. J., diss.—That sum is part of the profits Lord Campbell, C. J., diss.
of the occupation and would be received as such by
the hypothetical tenant :
the parochial principle does not exclude from the
rateable value of land " a profit derived from it by
the occupier, as occupier, in consideration of an
advantage derived from it in another parish."


(2). *The South Eastern Ry. Co.* v. *Overseers of Dorking*,[1] S. E. Ry. Co. v. Dorking.
(Feb. 1854).

The A. Co. constructed a branch line joining the main line Facts.
of the B. Co.  The B. Co. became the sole occupiers of the
A. line under a lease for 1000 years, at £41,000 per ann.
Subsequently the A. line and the B. line were amalgamated
by Act of Parliament, on the terms of the B. Co. paying the
shareholders of the A. Co. perpetual annuities to the amount
of £41,000.  Two rates were the subjects of appeal, one
made during the lease, and the other after the amalgamation.
The annual profits made on the A. line were less than
£41,000, but it was found as a fact in the case that the A.
line would be valuable as a feeder to other companies besides
the B. Co., and therefore if in the market might be an object of
competition among them.  The question was raised whether
the A. line was to be assessed in respect only of the net
profits earned upon it, or whether its value as a feeder was
to be taken into account also.

Held by Lord Campbell, C. J., Coleridge, and Crompton, Held C. V. rateable.
JJ. (diss. Erle, J.), that the value of the A. line as a feeder
was to be taken into account in assessing it.

Crompton, J.—Value as a feeder is profit derived from the Summary of judgments—
occupation ; would be an element in fixing the rent Crompton, J.

---

[1] 23 L. J. M. C. 84 ; 3 E. & B. 491.

of the hypothetical tenant ; and on principle increases the rateable value of the branch.

**Coleridge, J.**—Nothing is to be excluded which adds to the value of the occupation :

the question is not so much where the profits are produced as whether they are referable to the occupation : and,

rateable value within the parish may depend on matter without the parish.

**Lord Campbell, C. J.**—The parochial principle of ascertaining the value of the property within the parish, does not limit that value to the receipts for the use of it within the parish : feeder value originates in the parishes where the branch is, although the profits are actually received in the parishes on the main line.

**Erle, J., diss.**—It has been decided that the rateable value of a railway is to be determined by reference solely to the net profits earned within the parish : and,

if contributive value were rated the same profits would be rated twice over.

(3). *The London and North Western Ry. Co. v. Overseers of Cannock.*[1] (1863).

The branch line of the A. Co. joined the main line of the B. Co., and was leased to the latter Co. at a fixed rent. The A. line yielded no profit whatever as regards its own earnings, but it had a considerable value as a feeder to the B. line. The question for the opinion of the Court was, whether in rating the A. line its value as a feeder was to be taken into consideration.

*Marginal notes:* Coleridge, J. — Lord Campbell, C. J. — Erle, J., diss. — L. & N. W. Ry. Co. v. Cannock. — Facts.

---

[1] 9 L. T. N. S. 325.

The case was sent back by the Court in order that it Case remitted<br>to sessions. might be ascertained what "taking all its advantages into consideration" was the rateable value of the branch line in the respondent parish to the B. Co. No further judgments were delivered, but in the course of the argument it was said by,

> Cockburn, C. J.—" Rent is primâ facie evidence of value. Cockburn,<br>C. J. Suppose at this moment there were no lease and the appellants wanted to take it, what is the rent they would give? They would arrive at that by this process : What is the traffic on the branch, what are the expenses, what are the profits it would produce to the main line ? with some other considerations." [1] And by,

> Blackburn, J.—" What would be the elements of the rent ? Blackburn, J. why, amongst others, the capacity to add to the takings of the main line."

(4). *The Great Eastern Ry. Co.* v. *Overseers of Haughley.*[2] G. E. Ry. Co.<br>v. Haughley. (1866).

The question of contributive value was raised in this Facts. case in a slightly different way. The line under consideration ran from Norwich through Haughley and then through Ipswich to London. A train from Norwich to London would, after passing through Haughley, stop at Ipswich, where it would receive a large accession of traffic, and consequently in the parishes on the London side of Ipswich the net profit per train mile would be greater than in Haughley : the expense of running the train being the same in each case, but the earnings being greater where the train is better filled. An

---

[1] But Mellor, J., in *R.* v. *Llantrissant* (page 129, infra) said, " I think it must be taken that the Lord Chief Justice in the Haughley case did not quite adhere to the suggestion he threw out in the Cannock Case."

[2] L. R. 1 Q. B. 666 ; 35 L. J. M. C. 229.

individual passenger therefore, who is charged so much a
mile for the whole journey, would be carried at greater profit
to the Railway Co. between Ipswich and London than in
Haughley, and the profit per mile on carrying him the whole
journey would be greater than the profit per mile on carrying
him through Haughley. It was contended by the parish—

Contention of
the parish.
That each mile of railway over which traffic passes must be
regarded as contributing equally to the earning of the profits
derived from that traffic on the whole line of which that
mile is a part; in other words, that if the same traffic is
carried at a much greater profit over one part of the line
than over another, still each part of the line over which it is ·
carried must be considered as equally earning the profits
made on the whole journey, or that if the parish cannot
claim to share directly in the gross receipts beyond it, still
it would be entitled to take into account the additional
traffic beyond it as diminishing the expenses within it; and
that the fare of the through passenger being necessarily
received at one or the other end of the journey should be
apportioned equally over the length of the line in order to
ascertain the earnings in each parish, but that the expenses
ought not to be dealt with in a similar manner, because the
expense of conveying the passenger is not equal from one
end of the journey to the other, but varies inversely as the
amount of traffic.

Held C. V.
not rateable.
Held by Cockburn, C. J., Mellor and Shee, JJ., that in
assessing the line in Haughley no account was to be taken
of the traffic beyond the parish.

Summary of
judgments—
Cockburn,
C. J.
Cockburn, C. J.—The traffic beyond the parish if taken
into account at all must be in relation not to the
expenses, but to the profits; and, looked at as matter
of profit, it occurs beyond the parish of Haughley,
and it is an accident which affects the rateability
of the property where the profit accrues and not
elsewhere.

Mellor, J.—Rateable value in a parish is to be based on the actual profit earned there, and in this case the increased profit in the parishes on the London side of Haughley was not due to, or contributed by, the line in Haughley. He says: " I think that it is an accident to be assigned to the benefit of those parishes in which the accession of traffic takes place and not to a parish which has nothing to do with it."

Shee, J.—The contention of the parish involves the adop- tion of the mileage instead of the parochial principle, but the result of the authorities is that the parochial and not the mileage principle is to be applied to the rating of railways.

### (5). *R.* v. *Llantrissant.*[1]   (1869.)

The branch line of the A. Co. joined the line of the B. Co., and was leased to the latter at a fixed rent. The question for the opinion of the Court was whether in rating the A. line its value as a feeder to the B. line was to be taken into account.

Held by Mellor, J., Hannen and Hayes, JJ., concurring, that on the authority of the Haughley case the feeder value was not to be taken into account.

### (6). *R.* v. *London and North Western Railway Co.*[2] (1874.)

The B. Co. had become possessed of a branch line made by the A. Co., which communicated with the B. line, on the terms that the shareholders of the A. Co. should become stockholders in the B. Co. to the amount of the cost of con-

---

[1] L. R. 4 Q. B. 354 ; 38 L. J. M. C. 93.     [2] L. R. 9 Q. B. 134 ; s. c. *R.* v. *Bedford Union*, 43 L. J. M. C. 81.

struction of the A. line.  The A. line communicated with the lines of three other companies, and the B. Co., in order to divert traffic from those lines on to their own line, worked the A. line at very low fares, and consequently the profits actually earned upon the A. line were very small.  It was found as a fact in the case that the A. line would be valuable as a feeder to each of those companies, and that each of them would be willing, if it were in the market, to acquire it on the same terms as the B. Co. had done, and would then work it at similar low fares.

*Decision.*

*Competition to be taken into account.*

Held by Blackburn, Quain and Archibald, JJ., that the fact that there would be four competitors for the A. line in the market, each of whom would be willing to pay what was equivalent to a high rent for it, was an element to be taken into consideration in estimating its rateable value.

*C. V. rateable.*

This amounts to a decision in favour of the rateability of contributive value, because in holding that the high rent the competitors were as a fact willing to pay for the A. line on account of its value as a feeder, was to be taken in account, the judges imply that such rent was to be paid for something that was rateable.

*Summary of judgments—Blackburn, J.*

Blackburn, J.—The question is how much would the occupier get from the occupation enhanced by everything which his occupation would give him— here, since the line could be used as a feeder, it would have a contributive value—the question for the sessions is, what rent would be actually given if the line were in the market?

*Quain, J.*

Quain, J.—The value of the occupation is not merely what the railway earns in the particular parish, but something more in respect of its facility of communication with other railways.

*Archibald, J.*

Archibald, J.—Advantages that go along with the occupation are to be considered ; also the fact of competition.

(7). *The London and North Western Ry. Co.* v. *Irthlingborough.*[1] (1876.)

L. & N. W. Ry. Co. *v.* Irthlingborough.

A line, originally made by the A. Co., had subsequently been incorporated into the system of the B. Co. No profits were produced on the part of A. line within the parish in question, but it was found as a fact that if it were in the market it would fetch a certain yearly rent, as it would be a subject of competition among three main lines.

Facts.

Held by Blackburn and Quain, JJ., that the Quarter Sessions were right in taking the rent which they found to be obtainable for the line in the market as the basis of the rateable value of the part of the line within the parish.

Held C. V. rateable.

Blackburn, J.—This case is governed by *R.* v. *L. & N. W. Ry. Co.*,[2] which decided that "in consequence of the competition of other lines one element for fixing the rateable value was the enhanced traffic which the tenant would enjoy elsewhere."

Summary of judgments— Blackburn, J.

Quain, J.—The value of the piece of line in the parish is to be taken as enhanced by the more valuable traffic in other parishes.

Quain, J.

Now in order to rate an occupier on account of the contributive value of a branch line which he occupies, it must first be shown that it is part of the fruits of his occupation, or in other words that it would increase the value of the occupation to the hypothetical tenant. That is a question which depends on the particular circumstances of each case, but in cases similar to those under review it seems probable that the answer would be in the affirmative, having regard to the judgments of Lord Campbell, C. J., in *The Newmarket Case*,

Whether fruits of the occupation, depends on the circumstances of each case.

---

[1] 35 L. T. N. S. 327.   *Bedford Union*, 43 L. J. M. C. 81.
[2] L. R. 9 Q. B. 134 ; s. c. *R.* v.   See page 129, supra.

of Lord Campbell, C. J., Crompton and Coleridge, JJ., in *S. E. Ry. Co.* v. *Dorking*, of Cockburn, C. J., and Blackburn, J., in *L. & N. W. Ry. Co.* v. *Cannock*, of Blackburn, Quain, and Archibald, JJ., in *R.* v. *L. & N. W. Ry. Co.*, and of Blackburn and Quain, JJ., in *L. & N. W. Ry. Co.* v. *Irthlingborough*.

Finding of Coleridge and Erle, JJ., in the Newmarket case doubted.

Among the judges who held contributive value not rateable, Erle and Coleridge, JJ., alone, (in the Newmarket case), made it one of the grounds of their decision that the value of the occupation of the hypothetical tenant would not thereby be increased, and the correctness of the point of view from which they formed that opinion seems sufficiently doubtful to warrant a slight digression from the main subject, in order to examine into its weight as a precedent. They held that under the circumstances of that case, the guarantee was a collateral one, and would not necessarily pass to an incoming tenant. Erle, J., said, "If the purchaser of a farm had a guarantee that the rent should yield him £3 per cent. on the purchase money, the rateable value, that is, the rent which a tenant would pay for the farm, would not be increased by this collateral contract. Now the Newmarket shareholders are, in effect, the landlords, the Company are the tenants paying dividend for rent, and the Eastern Counties Co. are the guarantors, and the guarantee is irrelevant to the rateable value." Coleridge, J., said, "In point of fact, a lease of the line might very well be made, supposing the requisite powers, without involving a transfer of the benefit of this agreement to the lessee." On

Lord Campbell's view.

the other hand Lord Campbell, C. J., said in the same case, "If this branch was let to a tenant, he would be entitled under the agreement, and the Act of Parliament confirming it, to this contingent payment." In this particular case then (where, as Coleridge, J., said, the facts were very peculiar and could seldom form a precedent for any other), there was a difference of opinion as to whether the hypothetical tenant would enjoy the benefit of the guarantee which was given to the occupier in consideration of the contributive value of the

branch ; but it is submitted that the question should have ^True^ test.
been not so much whether the guarantee would *necessarily*
have passed to a lessee, or whether a lease *might have been*
made without including it, as whether it would have passed,
to use the expression of Lord Denman, C. J., in *R.* v. *G. W.
Ry. Co.* (1st case),[1] to a tenant " placed as occupier in the same
position as the party rated," and whether it should not be
treated as an element of a tenancy supposed for the purpose
"of ascertaining the existing value to the existing occupier." [2]

In *R.* v. *Fletton,*[3] Cockburn, C. J., says, " The true principle according to which the value of the occupation to the
hypothetical tenant contemplated by the Parochial Assessment Act is to be estimated, is to assume the continuance of
the circumstances which constitute the value to the existing
occupier, unless it be made to appear that those circumstances are about to undergo a change."

In *G. W. Ry. Co.* v. *Badgworth,*[4] it was said in argument
that the hypothetical tenant would not look at private bargains
between the two companies, but Cockburn, C. J., said, " Yes,
he would. The question is what he would give as rent under
existing circumstances." The reasoning of Coleridge and
Erle, JJ., in the Newmarket case (if correct) would not
apply to the more common case where the branch and the ^Where^ ^branch^
main line are in the same occupation, and where the hypo- ^and^ ^main^ ^line^
^in^ ^same^ ^occu-^
thetical tenant, being supposed to be tenant of one system ^pation^ ^the^
^Newmarket^
consisting of both, must consequently be supposed to receive ^case^ ^not^ ^a^
the profits of both; but it is submitted that even in such a ^precedent.^
case as the Newmarket one, a less restrictive view than theirs
should be taken of the advantages that would pass to the
hypothetical tenant.

---

[1] 15 L. J. M. C. 80; 6 Q. B. 179.   [3] 30 L. J. M. C. 89; 3 E. & E. 450.
[2] Per Lord Denman, C. J., in *R.* v.   [4] L. R. 2 Q. B. 251 ; 36 L. J. M. C.
*Grand Junction Railway Co.,* 13   33.
L. J. M. C. 94 ; 4 Q. B. 18.

Conflict of
cases.

The Dorking
and Cannock
cases.

The Haughley
and Llan-
trissant cases.

R. v. L. & N.
W. Ry. Co.,
and L. & N.
W. Ry. Co.
v. Irthling-
borough.

Authorities in
support of R.
v. Haughley.

If however it is found in a particular case that the value of a branch line as a feeder would influence the rent of the hypothetical tenant, then on the authority of *S. E. Ry. Co.* v. *Dorking* (though diss. Erle, J.) and *L. & N. W. Ry. Co.* v. *Cannock*, it would appear that he would be rateable in respect of it on the ground that it is part of the fruits of the occupation.

But then comes *G. E. Ry. Co.* v. *Haughley*, followed in *R.* v. *Llantrissant*, where while apparently not disputing that the contributive value was part of the fruits of the occupation, the judges adopted the view which Erle, J., had taken when dissenting in *S. E. Ry. Co.* v. *Dorking*, namely, that the fact that it is profit accruing out of the parish excludes it from rateability.

Finally, there are *R.* v. *L. & N. W. Ry. Co.* and *L. & N. W. Ry. Co.* v. *Irthlingborough*, in which contributive value is again held rateable, in spite of the limit laid down in the Haughley case to profits accruing within the parish.

Apart from the Haughley and Llantrissant cases, the rule on the subject of contributive value might be stated to be that where value as a feeder would influence the rent of the hypothetical tenant, then he is rateable in respect of it; but, with the Haughley case before us, it must be added that inconsistently with this view it has been held, that the parochial principle, as applied to railways (and presumably to other properties extending over more than one parish), limits the measure of rateability in each parish to the profits earned and expenses incurred within the parish. It is true that the facts of the Haughley case might perhaps distinguish it from the cases in which contributive value has been held rateable, but from the reasoning of the judges there, it appears probable that they would have decided the Dorking and Cannock cases differently from the way in which they were in fact decided, although they do not overrule them nominatim.

In the Haughley case the judges held that the application of the parochial principle to railways involves that a parish has no concern with profit accruing beyond it. How far is this supported by authority? With regard to properties extending over more than one parish it was held in *R.* v. *Kingswinford*,[1] in the case of a canal passing through several parishes, that the rateable value of the part within each parish was to be based directly on the profits actually derived from that part, and was not to be determined by what is called the mileage system, which assumes that the rateable value of the part in the parish is in the same proportion to the rateable value of the whole, as the length or extent of the part is to the length or extent of the whole. Following *R.* v. *Kingswinford* is *R.* v. *Lower Mitton*,[2] in which Bayley, J., says, "It is now fully established (*R.* v. *Milton*[3] and *R.* v. *Palmer*[4]), that the proprietors of a canal or navigation are rateable as occupiers of the land covered with water in the particular parish in which the land lies; and it follows from thence and it was so decided in *R.* v. *Kingswinford*, that they are rateable in each parish in proportion to the profit which that part of the land covered with water which lies in the parish produces. If it is more productive than other parts of the canal either because there is more traffic, or because larger tolls are due upon it, or because the outgoings and expenses there are less, it must be assessed at a higher proportionate value. . . . . . Whether the subject-matter of the occupation be productive in itself, or rendered productive by something brought from another parish, or by being used in conjunction with property in another parish, no difference is to be made in the mode of rating. Thus whether the water in a parish be brought from the same parish or another parish, whether conveyed in pipes or carts or by engines, makes no difference if the land in which it is placed

---

[1] 7 B. & C. 236 ; s. c. *R.* v. *Dudley Canal Co.*, 6 L. J. (O. S.) M. C. 3.
[2] 8 L. J. (O. S.) M. C. 57 ; 9 B. & C. 810.
[3] 3 B. & Ald. 112.
[4] 1 B. & C. 546.

be thereby rendered more valuable." By parity of reasoning it would seem to follow that whether traffic on a railway in a parish arises in the parish or is contributed by a line in another parish makes no difference to its rateability in the parish where its profits are enjoyed. Then there are some authorities quoted in the judgment of Erle, J., in *S. E. Ry. Co.* v. *Dorking*, at more length than in the Haughley case, namely, *R.* v. *G. W. Ry. Co.* (2nd case),[1] *R.* v. *L. B. & S. C. Ry Co.*, *R,* v. *S. E. Ry. Co.*, and *R.* v. *Midl. Ry. Co.*,[2] in which it was decided that the rateable value of a part of a railway within a parish is to be estimated with reference to the net profits earned in the parish, and not on the mileage system, because under it some parishes would benefit in respect of profits earned in others.

Contra.　The above authorities seem to support the limitation of rateable value to profits earned within the parish, which was laid down in the Haughley case, but in favour of a more extended view of the parochial principle there is the case of the Amwell Spring, *R.* v. *New River Co.*,[3] where the New River Co. were held rateable at £300 per annum for land containing the spring which formed the New River, it being found that the land without the spring was worth but £5 per annum, and that the higher amount was in respect of profits made by the company. by selling the water in other parishes. It was there held that it matters not whether the profits are received within or without the parish so long as the land to the occupation of which they are due is within the parish. In *G. W. Ry. Co.* v. *Badgworth*,[4] the A. Co. and B. Co. each paid half the cost of constructing a line from C. to D., and when finished, the half of the line nearest C.

---

[1] 21 L. J. M. C. 84; 15 Q. B. 379, 1085.

[2] 15 Q. B. 313.

[3] 1 M. & S. 503. But see the remarks of Wightman, J., on this case in *R.* v. *West Middlesex Waterworks Co.*, 28 L. J. M. C. 135; 1 E. & E. 716.

[4] L. R. 2 Q. B. 251; 36 L. J. M. C. 33.

became by agreement the property of the A. Co., and the half nearest D. the property of the B. Co. The A. Co. had running powers over the half of the line belonging to the B. Co., in return for granting the B. Co. running powers over their half. In rating the A. Co. it was held that the profits they made in the parish on their own line were to be regarded as enhanced by the right to run free over the half of the line belonging to the B. Co. The value of the right to run over the B. line would depend on the profits made on it, which are profits made out of the parish, though the means of making them was the occupation of the A. line within the parish.

The matter stands at present thus :—In the Haughley and Llantrissant cases it was held that contributive value is not rateable, because only profits earned within the parish can be taken into account, while in the Dorking and Cannock cases, before the Haughley case, and in *R.* v. *L. & N. W. Ry. Co.*, and *L. & N. W. Ry. Co.* v. *Irthlingborough*, (after the Haughley case), contributive value was held rateable. *Result of the cases on contributive value.*

In this somewhat uncertain state of the law it is perhaps consolatory to the parishes, that, while the Railway Companies have no motive for fighting the question again, since if their rating is increased in one parish on account of contributive value, it will be correspondingly diminished in another; they themselves have, as a rule, very little inducement to raise it, on account of the difficulty of ascertaining what the value of a line as a feeder really is. In the Dorking case, Crompton, J., said, " it may be difficult and not often worth while, to introduce this new element into account." Lord Campbell, C. J., said, " I would earnestly dissuade parishes from ever making any claim under this head, unless where upon clear evidence the claim can in point of fact be established ; " and Erle, J., in saying that, " as a generality cannot be tested without a specific application, I suggest that if a case is again brought up relating to these points, it should state specifically what is the railway profit arising out *Absence of inducement to either side to raise the question again.*

of the parish which is liable to be rated within it," directs
the attention of the parishes to the practical difficulty that
remains, even supposing the principle established in their
favour.[1]

## DISTINCTION BETWEEN DIRECTLY AND INDIRECTLY PRODUCTIVE PORTIONS OF A PROPERTY.

Examples.

There is a distinction between the directly and indirectly
productive parts of a property, which is best illustrated by
examples.

The profits of waterworks, for instance, are earned by
supplying water to the consumer. It matters not to the con-

Water pipes.

sumer how far the water has been carried in mains or pipes
before it is delivered to him at his house, or wherever else he
receives it; nor does a consumer who lives several miles
from the waterworks pay a higher price for the water supplied than one who lives next door to them. What is paid
for, in each case, is water, and not the transit of water.
Hence the pipes by which the transit of water to the consumer is effected cannot be regarded as a direct source of
profit to the waterworks. Still, being essential to the business of supplying water, they are indirectly productive of
profit.[2]

Gas pipes.

Similar remarks may be made as to the pipes of a gas
company.[3]

Railway
stations.

So, in the case of a railway, what the passenger pays for
is conveyance from one place to another; therefore the line,

---

[1] See also per Shee, J., in the
Haughley case.

[2] *R. v. West Middlesex Waterworks Co.*, 28 L. J. M. C. 135;

1 E. & E. 716.

[3] *R. v. Sheffield Gas Co.*, 32 L. J.
M. C. 169; 4 B. & S. 135.

and not the stations and other buildings, that are only ancillary to the traffic, is the <u>direct source of profit</u>. But <u>the stations</u>, &c., as being incidentally useful in doing that which is the equivalent for the fares paid by the public, are <u>indirect sources of profit</u>.[1]

Again, if a Bridge Company erect a bridge over a river, and make approach roads leading to it, and take tolls from those who pass over, the bridge itself is the direct source of the rateable value, the passage over the river being that which is paid for, while <u>the approaches only indirectly conduce to the production of profits</u>.[2]

Approaches to a bridge.

The above examples indicate a simple test by which to determine whether a particular portion of a property is directly or indirectly productive, namely to inquire <u>what it is the customer pays for</u>.

The test is, What is it that is paid for?

Other examples of <u>indirectly productive property</u> are the reservoirs, buildings, and other premises belonging to water-works,[3] the gasometers and manufacturing premises of gas-works,[4] and the warehouses, graving docks, timber sheds, workshops, &c., forming part of a dock system.[5]

Other examples of indirect sources of profit.

A canal lock, for passing through which no special toll or due is taken, would be <u>only indirectly productive</u>, but a lock for passing through which tolls are charged, is rateable on the basis of those tolls.[6] The distinction between such a lock and a railway station would appear to be that in the case of the station <u>no separate charge is made for its use</u>, but

---

[1] *South Wales Railway Co.* v. *Swansea,* 24 L. J. M. C. 30 ; 4 E. & B. 189 ; *R.* v. *Grand Junction Railway Co.,* 13 L. J. M. C. 94 ; 4 Q. B. 18.

[2] *R.* v. *Hammersmith Bridge Co.,* 18 L. J. M. C. 85 : 15 Q. B. 369.

[3] *R.* v. *Bath,* (*Corporation of*), 14 East, 609 ; *R.* v. *West Middlesex Waterworks Co.,* 28 L. J. M. C. 135 ;

1 E. & E. 716.

[4] *R.* v. *Sheffield Gas Co.,* 32 L. J. M. C. 169 ; 4 B. & S. 135 ; *R.* v. *Cambridge Gas Co.,* 7 L. J. M. C. 50 ; 8 A. & E. 73.

[5] *Mersey Docks and Harbour Board* v. *Birkenhead,* L. R. 8 Q. B. 445 ; 42 L. J. M. C. 141.

[6] *R.* v. *Lower Mitton,* 8 L. J. (O. S.) M. C. 57 ; 9 B. & C. 810.

the gross charge made includes both the transit and the use of the station.[1]

**1st. The direct to be distinguished from the indirect sources of profit.**   The distinction between direct and indirect sources of profit is of importance wherever a property extends over more than one parish. If the entirety can be divided into two parts by separating the directly from the indirectly productive portions, such a division is to be made. This is both recognised in practice and based on authority.[2]

**2nd. The indirectly productive portions to be separately rated on their value to the concern.**   The indirectly productive portions are then to be separately rated. Each parish must rate the indirectly producing part that lies within it on an estimate of the rent it would yield regarded as a separate hereditament, but such estimate must be made not of its value per se as land, building, or whatever it may be, nor according to its original cost, but, in accordance with the principle of rebus sic stantibus, of the (probably enhanced) value which it possesses while used for the purpose for which it actually is used, and as a portion of the concern of which it in fact forms part.[3] A station, for instance, is not to be estimated merely at what any one would give for it as a building of a certain size, but at what the railway company might reasonably be expected to give for it in order to use it as part of their system, supposing it belonged to somebody else.

**3rd. In assessing the directly**   The indirectly productive parts of a concern having

---

[1] *R.* v. *Eastern Counties Railway Co.*, 32 L. J. M. C. 174 ; 4 B. & S. 58.

[2] *R.* v. *Hammersmith Bridge Co.*, 18 L. J. M. C. 85 ; 15 Q. B. 369 ; *R.* v. *Great Western Railway Co.*, (1st case) 15 L. J. M. C. 80 ; 6 Q. B. 179 ; *R.* v. *Mile End Old Town*, 16 L. J. M. C. 184 ; 10 Q. B. 208 ; *South Wales Railway Co.* v. *Swansea*, 24 L. J. M. C. 30 ; 4 E. & B. 189 ; *R.* v. *Eastern Counties Railway Co.*, 32 L. J. M. C. 174 ; 4 B. & S. 58.

[3] *R.* v. *London & South Western Railway Co.*, 11 L. J. M. C. 93, at 100; 1 Q. B. 558, at 584 ; *R.* v. *Mile End Old Town*, 16 L. J. M. C. 184 ; 10 Q. B. 208 ; *R.* v. *West Middlesex Waterworks Co.*, 28 L. J. M. C. 135 ; 1 E. & E. 716 ; *R.* v. *Sheffield Gas Co.*, 32 L. J. M. C. 169 ; 4 B. & S. 135 ; *R.* v. *North Staffordshire Railway Co.*, 30 L. J. M. C. 68 ; 3 E. & E. 392.

been rated on the above principle in the parishes within producing portion the value of the indirect is to be treated as a deduction. which they lie, their estimated annual value is then to be deducted, under the head of expenses, from the gross value of the directly productive portion, and the net profits remaining after this, and the other legitimate deductions, are then to be apportioned, for rating purposes, between the various parishes which contain any of the directly productive parts of the concern, in the proportion in which those net profits are earned in each of those parishes.[1]

In *R. v. Cambridge Gas Co.*,[2] the rateable value was ap- R. v. Cambridge Gas Co. portioned in the ratio of the quantity of apparatus in each parish, but this seems to have been on the assumption that it was impossible to suppose any superiority in one part of the apparatus over another, and that therefore the quantity of apparatus and the net profits in a parish would be in the same ratio. If this were so, it would have been one of the cases where the mileage system and the parochial principle give the same result, and so the mileage system may be used for the purpose of calculation.

## THE RATING OF RAILWAYS, CANALS AND DOCKS, GAS, WATER, AND TRAMWAY COMPANIES.

It will be desirable to supplement the general principles which have been elucidated in the foregoing pages with some remarks on the rating of various descriptions of property, beginning with that of railways, as being the most complicated.

---

[1] *R. v. Mile End Old Town*, 16 L. J. M. C. 184 ; 10 Q. B. 208 ; *R. v. Hammersmith Bridge Co.*, 18 L. J. M. C. 85 ; 15 Q. B. 369 ; *R. v. West Middlesex Waterworks Co.*, 28 L. J. M. C. 135 ; 1 E. & E. 716 ; *R. v. Sheffield Gas Co.*, 32 L. J. M. C. 169 ; 4 B. & S. 135.

[2] 7 L. J. M. C. 50 ; 8 A. & E. 73.

## RAILWAYS.[1]

Railway rating.
Trade Profits are not rateable, and yet railways are practically rated upon their Trade Profits; but the explanation of this apparent contradiction is that it is <u>as occupiers of land</u> that railway companies are rated, and their profits, being due to the occupation, become rateable <u>by the principle of enhanced value</u>.[2] Each parish must rate, as if it were a separate hereditament, the part of a railway lying within it,[3]

Rent of the hypothetical tenant,
upon an estimate of its net annual value, that is to say, of the rent, subject to certain deductions, at which it might reasonably be expected to let on a yearly tenancy. This appears difficult to carry out in practice, for it seems to require the assumption of such an improbable state of things as that a person could be found who would be willing to take, as tenant from year to year, the portion of a railway that lies in a single parish, and no more. This, as Lord Campbell, C. J., said in *R.* v. *G. W. Ry. Co.*,[4] is "an improbable and almost absurd supposition," and there is no such state of things in actual existence ; but what we do find is that a railway company works its system as a whole, and keeps detailed accounts of all its incomings

arrived at by analysis of the balance sheet.
and outgoings ; and by sorting out, so to speak, the items in those accounts, and classifying them under such heads as the Parochial Assessment Act and the established rules of rating suggest, we are enabled to eliminate from them the amount

Gross Estimated Rental or Gross Value.
which represents the rent a hypothetical tenant, holding on the terms of the Parochial Assessment Act, would give for the part of the railway in the parish, and also the amount of the deductions to be made under that Act from the rent, in

Rateable Value.
order to give the rateable value.

---

[1] The importance of this branch of the subject may be estimated by the fact that the twelve principal railway companies alone pay nearly one-tenth of the whole sum levied in rates in England and Wales. See Land, Vol.

v., page 114.

[2] See pages 99 and 100 supra.

[3] Parochial Assessment Act, 6 & 7 Will. IV., c. 96.

[4] 21 L. J. M. C. 84 ; 15 Q. B. 379, 1085.

This may be done somewhat in the following manner :—

RATEABLE VALUE OF THE A. B. RAILWAY IN THE PARISH OF C.
FOR THE YEAR 1883.

| | | | |
|---|---|---:|---:|
| I. Gross Receipts . . . . . . | | | £35,000[1] |
| II. Working Expenses— | | | |
| (a) Locomotive, carriage, and wagon . | . £9,000 | | |
| (b) Traffic charges . . . . . | 7,000 | | |
| (c) Repairs of rolling stock . . . . | 200 | | |
| (d) Repairs of permanent way . . . | 300 | | |
| (e) General charges . . . . . | 150 | | |
| (f) Law charges . . . . . . | 50 | | |
| (g) Government duty . . . . . | 800 | | |
| (h) Rates and taxes (5s. in the £ on an assessment of £3,600) . . . . | 900 | | |
| | £18,400 | 18,400 | |
| | | 16,600 | |
| III. Indirectly Productive Portions of the Property— | | | |
| Rateable value of stations separately assessed | £2,000 | 2,000 | |
| | | 14,600 | |
| IV. Tenant's Deductions, or Occupier's Share— | | | |
| (a) Interest on capital—5 p. c. on £30,000 . | 1,500 | | |
| (b) Depreciation of rolling stock, &c. . . | 1,700 | | |
| (c) Risks and casualties—2½ p. c. on £30,000 | 750 | | |
| (d) Interest on working capital—5 p. c. on £1,000 . . . . . . . | 50 | | |
| (e) Tenant's profits—10 p. c. on £30,000 . | 3,000 | | |
| | £7,000 | 7,000 | |
| **Gross Estimated Rental, or Gross Value**[2] | | 7,600 | |
| V. Landlord's Deductions, or Statutable Deductions— | | | |
| Renewal of way and insurance . . . £4,000 | | 4,000 | |
| **Rateable Value** . . . . . | | £3,600 | |

[1] The figures are merely fictitious ones introduced by way of illustration.

[2] 'Gross Estimated Rental' is the term used in the schedules to the P. A. Act of 1836, and the Union Assessment Committee Act of 1862 (25 & 26 Vict. c. 103).

The former of those Acts did not

The system
applicable
to other
properties as
well as rail-
ways.

The above is, as some of the subdivisions show intended primarily as an example of railway rating, but the rateable value of canals, docks, gas, water, and tramway companies, &c., may be ascertained in the same manner, by arranging under the five main heads, namely, (1) gross receipts ; (2) working expenses ; (3) indirect sources of profits ; (4) tenant's deductions, and (5) landlord's deductions, the amounts properly belonging to each, and substituting for such subdivisions as locomotive expenses, the corresponding items which are found to exist in the case of those undertakings. The system is equally applicable whether the whole concern, as may be the case with docks, or only a part of it, as in the case of a railway, is within the parish. In

---

give a definition of 'Gross Estimated Rental,' but the latter (by sec. 15), defined it as "the rent at which the hereditament might reasonably be expected to let from year to year, free of all usual tenant's rates and taxes, and tithe commutation rent-charge, if any." But the rating of property within the Metropolis is now regulated by the Metropolis Valuation Act of 1869 (32 & 33 Vict. c. 67), in the 1st schedule to which the term 'Gross Value' is used in place of 'Gross Estimated Rental.' That Act defines 'Gross Value' as "the annual rent which a tenant might reasonably be expected, taking one year with another, to pay for an hereditament, if the tenant undertook to pay all usual tenant's rates and taxes and tithe commutation rent-charge if any, and if the landlord undertook to bear the cost of the repairs, and insurance, and the other expenses, if any, necessary to maintain the hereditament in a state to command that rent." It defines

'Rateable Value,' as "the gross value after deducting therefrom the probable annual average cost of the repairs, insurance, and other expenses as aforesaid."

These definitions may be regarded as applicable to property without, as well as within, the Metropolis (although the Bill of the same year which dealt with property outside the Metropolis, the Valuation of Property Bill, 1869, which also contained these definitions, was withdrawn and therefore did not become law), for the Metropolis Valuation Act did not contain any new principle, but was merely an endeavour to facilitate the carrying out of the existing law, by inter alia giving "a better definition of Gross Estimated Rental" to which it gave the name of 'Gross Value.' (See Hansard, Vol. cxciv. page 171). This "better definition," it will be noticed, avoids the ambiguity involved in the words "free of" in the former one.

the latter case the apportionment to the parish of its share of the various items must be calculated in accordance with the parochial principle.

I. GROSS RECEIPTS.—The gross receipts of railways include[1] all fares for the conveyance of passengers, receipts for the carriage of goods and cattle, tolls, if any, received for the use of the line,[2] and payments for user of line or stations by other companies.[3] All these are to be reckoned at the amounts actually charged by the company, not at the maximum their statute allows them to charge.[4] Passenger and goods receipts are not to be for rating purposes separated, (as they are by the Railway Clearing House for other purposes), into what is due for the use of the line, and what for the use of stations, &c., (i.e. terminals); but all that is earned, whether by the stations or by the line, is to be reckoned in the general profits of the concern; therefore gross charges covering the use of both line and stations come in their entirety under the heading of receipts.[5] Besides what is actually received in money, there is to be included among gross receipts the money value of anything earned by means of the occupation, which is paid in another way than in money; as, for instance, where a line of railway belonged to two companies, each owning half the line, and receiving from the other company running powers free over the other half, in return for the grant of a similar privilege over its own half, neither company receiving payment in money for the

*Margin notes:* Gross receipts—Fares. Tolls. Rents. Terminals. Earnings in kind.

---

[1] *R.* v. *London & South Western Railway Co.*, 11 L. J. M. C. 93; 1 Q. B. 558; *R.* v. *Grand Junction Railway Co.*, 13 L. J. M. C. 94; 4 Q. B. 18.

[2] When railways were first made it was contemplated that other persons besides the railway company would act as carriers on the line, paying tolls to the company for the user of it.

[3] *R.* v. *Fletton*, 30 L. J. M. C. 89; 3 E. & E. 450; *R.* v. *Sherard (Lord)*, 33 L. J. M. C. 5.

[4] *R.* v. *Stockton & Darlington Railway Co.*, 8 L. T. N. S. 422.

[5] *R.* v. *Eastern Counties Railway Co.*, 32 L. J. M. C. 174; 4 B. & S. 58.

running powers it granted to the other over its own half because they were paid for by the grant of corresponding powers over the other half; it was held that the receipts of each company included what the other would have paid in money for the running powers if it had not paid for them in another way.[1] But where, under the system of through tickets, the company issuing the ticket, and on whose line the journey commences, have to hand over a portion of the fare received to the other company, on whose line the latter part of the journey is performed, this portion does not form part of the gross receipts of the first mentioned company; it is a part of the receipts of the latter company, which, for the convenience of all parties, the former company receives for them.[2]

*Through tickets.*

II. WORKING EXPENSES.—(a.) **Locomotive, Carriage, and Wagon Expenses.**—The cost of running the passenger and goods trains should be apportioned in the ratio of the number of train-miles of each description run in the parish. (b.) **Traffic Charges** are to be allocated in proportion to the traffic receipts of the line in the parish. (c.) **Repairs of Rolling Stock.**—This item strictly belongs to the head of Tenant's Deductions, but it is commonly placed among working expenses. (d.) **Repairs of the Permanent Way.**—This too is usually placed here, though it is one of the Landlord's Deductions. The actual outlay in the parish should be ascertained; apportionment on the mileage system is not allowable.[3] (e.) **General Charges**[4] include central superintendence, the salaries of directors, superintendents, clerks,

*Working expenses— Locomotive, carriage and wagon.*

*Traffic charges.*

*Repairs of rolling stock.*

*Repairs of permanent way.*

*General charges.*

---

[1] *Great Western Railway Co.* v. *Badgworth*, L. R. 2 Q. B. 251; 36 L. J. M. C. 33. See also *R.* v. *London Brighton & South Coast Railway Co.*, 20 L. J. M. C. 124; 15 Q. B. 313.

[2] *R.* v. *St. Pancras (Vestry of)*, 32 L. J. M. C. 146; 3 B. & S. 810.

[3] *London & North Western Railway Co.* v. *King's Norton*, 34 J. P. 102.

[4] *R.* v. *Southampton Dock Co.*, 20 L. J. M. C. 155; 14 Q. B. 587; *R.* v. *Great Western Railway Co.* (1st case), 15 L. J. M. C. 80; 6 Q. B. 179.

&c. But where Docks were managed by unpaid commis- sioners no deduction for expenses of direction was allowed.[1] (f.) **Law Charges** should be distributed in proportion to receipts. They do not include any allowance for interest on the preliminary expenses of forming the company, ob- taining the Act of Parliament, &c.[2] (g.) **Government Duty**[3] (see 5 & 6 Vict. c. 79, and 7 & 8 Vict. c. 85, s. 9) should be apportioned in the ratio of the receipts from Passenger Traffic in the parish, exclusive of Parliamentary Fares. (h.) **Rates and Taxes.**—Tithe Commutation Rent-charge.— Rates and Taxes include 'all usual tenant's rates and taxes',[4] such as Poor Rate,[5] General Rate, Tenant's Property Tax[6] (but not Landlord's Property Tax), and Sewers Rate,[7] (but not a voluntary Water Rate).[8] No deduction is to be made for income tax on Tenant's Profits.[9] The allowance for Rates and Taxes ought to be made upon the net rateable value after the Rates and Taxes themselves, in addition to all other proper allowances, have been deducted.[10] Tithe Commutation Rent-charge is a deduction under the Paro- chial Assessment Act; but in cases where tithe has been

*Margin notes:* Law charges. Government duty. Rates and taxes—Tithe commutation rent-charge.

---

[1] *Tyne Improvement Commissioners* v. *Cherton,* 1 E. & E. 516 ; s. c. *R.* v. *Cherton,* 32 L. J. M. C. 192; s. c. *R.* v. *Tyne Improvement Commissioners,* 6 L. T. N. S. 489.

[2] *R.* v. *Great Western Railway Co.* (1st case), 15 L. J. M. C. 80 ; 6 Q. B. 197.

[3] *Attorney-General* v. *Oxford, Wor- cester & Wolverhampton Railway Co.,* 31 L. J. Ex. 18.

[4] Parochial Assessment Act, 6 & 7 Will. IV. c. 96, s. 1.

[5] *R.* v. *Hull Dock Co.,* 3 B. & C. 516 ; 5 Dow. & Ry. 359 ; (decided be- fore the P. A. Act).

[6] *R.* v. *Great Western Railway*

*Co.* (1st case) 15 L. J. M. C. 80 ; 6 Q. B. 179 ; *R.* v. *Goodchild,* 27 L. J. M. C. 233; E. B. & E. 1 ; but see *R.* v. *Southampton Dock Co.,* 20 L. J. M. C. 155 ; 14 Q. B. 587.

[7] *R.* v. *Hall Dare,* 34 L. J. M. C. 17 ; 5 B. & S. 785 ; *R.* v. *Adames,* 2 L. J. M. C. 90 ; 4 B. & Ad. 61.

[8] *R.* v. *Bilston,* (2nd case) L. R. 1 Q. B. 18 ; 35 L. J. M. C. 73.

[9] *R.* v. *Southampton Dock Co.,* 20 L. J. M. C. 155 ; 14 Q. B. 587.

[10] *Tyne Improvement Commissioners* v. *Cherton,* 1 E. & E. 516 ; s. c. *R.* v. *Cherton,* 32 L. J. M. C. 192; s. c. *R.* v. *Tyne Improvement Commissioners,* 6 L. T. N. S. 489.

commuted for a payment free of poor rate, so that the vicar is not rateable, then such payment is not to be deducted in estimating the value of the property to the occupier.[1]

*Indirect sources of profit—*

III. INDIRECT SOURCES OF PROFIT.—We have already seen, (pages 138 to 141, supra,) that the indirectly productive parts of a property are to be rated separately ; their earnings going to swell the general receipts of the concern, and a sum representing a reasonable rent for those portions of the property being charged among the general outgoings. This applies to the stations of a railway company. As to what a station includes, see *L. & N. W. Ry. Co. v. Wigan.*[2]

*Stations.*

*Tenant's deductions— Interest on capital.*

IV. TENANT'S DEDUCTIONS, or Occupier's Share.—(a.) Interest on capital.—The tenant of a railway would be obliged, in order to work it, to invest a certain amount of capital in rolling stock and tenant's fixtures, and he could not say he had made a profit until he had been paid the interest on that capital. A percentage, (say 5 per cent.,) on the sum representing tenant's capital, forms therefore the first item under the head of Tenant's Deductions.[3] But the value of such machinery and plant as would be landlord's fixtures, is not to be included in tenant's capital.[4] The percentage is to be calculated not on the amount of capital that was actually invested by the company in rolling stock, &c., but on the amount which an incoming tenant taking that stock at a valuation in its existing condition would have to pay

---

[1] *Hackett v. Long Bennington*, 33 L. J. M. C. 137 ; 16 C. B. N. S. 38.

[2] 2 Nev. & Macn. 240.

[3] *R. v. Grand Junction Railway Co.*, 13 L. J. M. C. 94 ; 4 Q. B. 18; *R. v. Great Western Railway Co.* (1st case), 15 L. J. M. C. 80 ; 6 Q. B. 179 ; *R. v. London, Brighton & South Coast Railway Co.*, 20 L. J. M. C. 124 ; 15 Q. B. 313.

[4] As to the distinction between landlord's and tenant's fixtures, see *R. v. North Staffordshire Railway Co.*, 30 L. J. M. C. 68 ; 3 E. & E. 392 ; *R. v. Lee*, L. R. 1 Q. B. 241 ; 35 L. J. M. C. 105 ; *R. v. Halstead*, 32 J. P. 118 ; *Chidley v. West Ham*, 35 L. T. N. S. 486 ; 39 J. P. 310 ; *Laing v. Bishopwearmouth*, 3 Q. B. D. 299 ; 47 L. J. M. C. 41 ; and the other cases referred to at p. 109 et seq. supra, under Enhancement by Fixtures.

for it.[1]  **(b.) Depreciation of Rolling Stock, &c.**—As the per-centage for interest on capital is to be calculated, not on the cost price of the rolling stock, but on the value which that stock bears at the time the rate is made, and as that value is probably a depreciated one, for there is a constant depreciation in the stock over and above that which is compensated for by the actual repairs done to it, (the cost of which has been placed under Working Expenses,) an allowance must be made for this depreciation,[2] under which a portion of the capital with which the tenant came in vanishes every year, before a residue which is really all profit can be reached. **(c.) Risks and Casualties.**—See *R. v. G. W. Ry. Co.* (1st case),[3] and *Manchester, Sheffield, & Lincolnshire Ry. Co. v. Caistor Union.*[4] **(d.) Interest on Working Capital.**—See *Manchester, Sheffield, & Lincolnshire Ry. Co. v. Caistor Union,*[5] *R. v. North Staffordshire Ry. Co.,*[6] and *Tyne Improvement Commissioners v. Cherton.*[7] **(e.) Tenant's Profits.** —After having made all the foregoing deductions we must, before we can get at the rent the hypothetical tenant would pay, further deduct from the balance of Gross Receipts still remaining, a sum on account of Tenant's Profits,[8] for no tenant would be willing to pay to the landlord a rent equal to the entire balance of receipts over expenses. A man would decline to become a tenant at all on those terms ; he

*Margin notes:* Depreciation of rolling stock. Risks and casualties. Interest on working capital. Tenant's profits.

---

[1] *R. v. Great Western Railway Co.* (1st case), 15 L. J. M. C. 80 ; 6 Q. B. 179 ; *R. v. North Staffordshire Railway Co.*, 30 L. J. M. C. 68 ; 3 E. & E. 392 ; *Manchester, Sheffield & Lincolnshire Railway Co. v. Caistor Union*, 2 Nev. & Macn. 53, at 67.

[2] *R. v. Great Western Railway Co.* (2nd case), 21 L. J. M. C. 90 ; 15 Q. B. 379, 1085 ; *Great Eastern Railway Co. v. Haughley*, L. R. 1 Q. B. 666 ; 35 L. J. M. C. 229.

[3] 15 L. J. M. C. 80 ; 6 Q. B. 179.

[4] 2 Nev. & Macn. 53, at 67.

[5] Ib.

[6] 30 L. J. M. C. 68 ; 3 E. & E. 392.

[7] 1 E. & E. 516 ; s. c. *R. v. Cherton*, 32 L. J. M. C. 192 ; s. c. *R. v. Tyne Improvement Commissioners*, 6 L. T. N. S. 489.

[8] *R. v. Grand Junction Railway Co.*, 13 L. J. M. C. 94 ; 4 Q. B. 18 ; *R. v. Great Western Railway Co.*, (1st case), 15 L. J. M. C. 80 ; 6 Q. B. 179 ; *R. v. North Staffordshire Railway Co.*, 30 L. J. M. C. 68 ; 3 E. & E. 392.

would not undertake the trouble of management unless he expected to get some profit out of the undertaking. In estimating the amount to be allocated to Tenant's Profits we must consider, firstly, what amount of capital the tenant would have to invest, and, secondly, what percentage of profit would be reasonably sufficient to induce a person to become tenant of such a concern as the one in question. But if from the nature of the circumstances existing in a particular case the supposition of a tenant in receipt of profit is the supposition of an impossibility, then no allowance should be made for Tenant's Profits.[1]

Landlord's deductions—

V. LANDLORD'S DEDUCTIONS, or Statutable Deductions.— The balance of Gross Receipts remaining after all the above mentioned deductions represents the amount of rent which a tenant would pay. But from this there are what are called Landlord's Deductions to be made before we arrive at the rateable value. Under the Parochial Assessment Act there are to be deducted from the rent the probable average an-

Insurance.

nual cost of the repairs, insurance, and other expenses, if any, necessary to maintain the property in a state to com-

Renewal of way.

mand the rent. **Renewal of Way.**—Maintenance of Way, viz., the ordinary repairs done to it, is usually placed under the head of Working Expenses, though it really is a Landlord's Deduction ; but over and above the item of maintenance of way, the landlord is entitled to an allowance under the head of Renewal of Way. For just as an allowance is made to the tenant for depreciation of rolling stock in addition to an allowance for its annual repair, so must an allowance be made to the landlord to countervail the gradual depreciation of the way, and the consequent necessity for its renewal from time to time if it is to continue to command the rent.[2] The allowance is to

---

[1] *Mersey Docks and Harbour Board v. Liverpool,* L. R. 9 Q. B. 84 ; 43 L. J. M. C. 33.

[2] *R.* v. *Grand Junction Railway Co.,* 13 L. J. M. C. 94 ; 4 Q. B. 18 ; *R.* v. *Great Western Railway Co.*

be not of the actual expenditure in the year when renewal is effected, but of the annual expenditure on the average.[1]

DEDUCTIONS NOT ALLOWABLE.—No deduction is to be made for interest on borrowed money,[2] or on the preliminary outlay in the formation and promotion of the company,[3] or for goodwill.[4] Rent is not a deduction:[5] if it were there would be nothing to rate. Deductions not allowable.

**Deficiency in rates during construction.**—While a railway is in course of construction, the land taken for the purpose would not be rateable on general principles, because during that time the occupation yields no profit. But it is specially provided by the 133rd section of the Lands Clauses Consolidation Act[6]—and similar provisions are often found in the private Acts of railways—that until the works are completed and assessed to the poor rate the promoters shall be liable to make good the deficiency in the rates caused by their having rendered for a time unprofitable, and therefore not rateable, the lands taken by them. The measure of the deficiency is to be the rental at the time of the passing of the special Act. 'Until the works are completed and assessed,' does not mean until the entire system of railways, or other works, authorised by the special Act are completed, but until the portion within the parish is complete and assessable.[7] Deficiency in rates during construction of railway.

---

(1st case), 15 L. J. M. C. 80 ; 6 Q. B. 179 ; *R. v. London, Brighton & South Coast Railway Co.*, 20 L. J. M. C. 124 ; 15 Q. B. 313 ; *R. v. Great Western Railway Co.* (2nd case), 21 L. J. M. C. 90 ; 15 Q. B. 379, 1085 ; *R. v. Wells*, L. R. 2 Q. B. 542 ; 36 L. J. M. C. 109.

[1] *Mersey Docks and Harbour Board v. Liverpool*, L. R. 9 Q. B. 84 ; 43 L. J. M. C. 33.

[2] *R. v. Chaplin*, 1 B. & Ad. 926 ; *R. v. Blackfriars Bridge Co.*, 8 L. J. M. C. 29 ; 9 A. & E. 828 ; *R. v.*

*Holme Reservoirs*, 29 J. P. 165 ; *Mersey Docks v. Liverpool*, L. R. 9 Q. B. 84 ; L. J. M. C.

[3] *R. v. Great Western Railway Co.* (1st case), 15 L. J. M. C. 80 ; 6 Q. B. 179.

[4] *R. v. Grand Junction Railway Co.*, 13 L. J. M. C. 94 ; 4 Q. B. 18. See also *R. v. Mile End Old Town*, 16 L. J. M. C. 184 ; 10 Q. B. 208.

[5] *R. v. Parrott*, 5 T. R. 593 ; *R. v. Chaplin*, 1 B. & Ad. 926.

[6] 8 & 9 Vict. c. 18.

[7] *East London Railway Co.* v.

'Liable to make good the deficiency,' means, not that the promoters are to be rated, but, that they are to be liable in an action brought to recover the amount of the deficiency.[1] Other points arising on the section are discussed and determined in *Stratton* v. *Metropolitan Board of Works.*[2]

## CANALS.

Canals.<br>Private Acts.

Canals are as a rule rateable, like railways, by the method which has just been explained ; but it has sometimes been provided by <u>private or local acts</u>, that <u>certain canals should be rated in the same proportion as the adjacent lands,</u> instead of on the basis of their actual profits.

Value at time of rate not at date of the Act.

When such a provision exists, the standard of value to be taken is not the value of the adjacent lands at the date of the Act, <u>but their value at the time of the rate.</u>[3]

Where separate mention of land and buildings.

Where the Act mentions separately the land and the buildings of the Canal Company, enacting that their land is to be rated like other land, and their buildings like other buildings, adjacent or near or in the parish as the case may be, it seems that the land covered by the water of the canal is to be rated at the value of <u>land not built on,</u> even though it would in all human probability have been built on if the canal had not been made.[4]

Where no separate mention of buildings.

But where no separate mention is made in the Act of the buildings of the Canal Company, but it is merely stated that the Company are to be rated for the lands taken in pursuance of the Act in the same proportion as adjacent lands,[5] then it is not to be inferred that they cannot

---

*Whitechurch,* L. R. 7 H. L. 81 ; 43 L. J. M. C. 159 ; overruling *R.* v. *Metropolitan District Railway Co.,* L. R. 6 Q. B. 698; 40 L. J. M. C. 113.

[1] *London (Mayor of)* v. *St. Andrew, Holborn,* L. R. 2 C. P. 574 ; 36 L. J. M. C. 95 ; *Wheeler* v. *Metropolitan Board of Works,* L. R. 4 Ex. 303 ;

38 L. J. Ex. 165.

[2] L. R. 10 C. P. 76 ; 44 L. J. M. C. 33.

[3] *R.* v. *Monmouthshire Canal Co.,* 3 A. & E. 619.

[4] *Regent's Canal Co.* v. *St. Pancras,* 3 Q. B. D. 73 ; 47 L. J. M. C. 37.

[5] *R.* v. *Glamorganshire Canal Co.,* 29 L. J. M. C. 238 ; 3 E. & E. 186.

be rated at a higher value than that of mere land unbuilt on;
on the contrary, the standard of value is to be, not the
nearest agricultural land, but the nearest land of any description, and there must be brought into hotchpot all the adjacent   Hotchpot.
lands, built on as well as unbuilt on, and the average value
taken of all the lands so brought into hotchpot, which value
will of course vary in proportion to the quantity of land that
is built on.

The above seem to be the general principles established
by the cases[1] bearing on provisions of this nature, but it
must be borne in mind that the language of the statutes
respectively in question, is not precisely the same in each
case.

Locks on a canal seem *similar* analogous to stations on a railway,   Locks.
but the question whether locks are to be rated in the same
way as stations, is not left by the reported decisions in a
satisfactory condition. In *R.* v. *Lower Mitton*,[2] it was held
that a lock was to be rated like any other portion of the
canal, the lock dues being therefore to be treated as a
parochial earning, and not included in the general receipts of
the undertaking like station earnings; but in a more recent
case, *R.* v. *Coventry Canal Co.*,[3] it was held that the expenses of a lock were not to be regarded as parochial expenses,
but were to be thrown on the whole line of the canal. These   Decisions in-
cases seem inconsistent, for if the lock dues are to be credited   consistent;
                                                                  but should

---

[1] *R.* v. *Grand Junction Canal Co.*,
1 B. & Ald. 289; *R.* v. *St. Peter the
Great, Worcester*, 5 B. & C. 473;
*R.* v. *Monmouthshire Canal Co.*, 3
A. & E. 619; *R.* v. *Chelmer &
Blackwater Navigation Co.*, 2 B. &
Ad. 14; *R.* v. *Grand Junction Canal
Co.*, 7 W. R. 597 (cf. *Grand Junction
Canal Co.* v. *Hemel Hempstead*,
infra); *R.* v. *Glamorganshire Canal
Co.*, 29 L. J. M. C. 238; 3 E. & E.

186; *Grand Junction Canal Co.* v.
*Hemel Hempstead*, L. R. 6 Q. B. 173;
40 L. J. M. C. 25; *Warwick &
Birmingham Canal Co.* v. *Birmingham*, 27 L. T. N. S. 487; *Regent's
Canal Co.* v. *St. Pancras*, 3 Q. B. D.
73; 47 L. J. M. C. 37.

[2] 8 L. J. (O. S.) M. C. 57; 9 B. &
C. 810.

[3] 28 L. J. M. C. 102; 1 E. & E.
572.

probably be
treated as in-
direct sources
of profit like
railway
stations.

entirely to the line in the parish, why are not likewise the expenses of the lock? and if the expenses of the lock are thrown on the whole line, why should not also the receipts of the lock be treated as receipts of the canal as a whole? It is submitted that the decision in *R.* v. *Coventry Canal Co.*, is the one to be preferred, and that locks should be treated as indirect sources of profit like stations.

## DOCKS.

Docks.

For a table of receipts and deductions in the case of a Dock Company see *R.* v. *Southampton Dock Co.*[1] It sometimes happens that in consideration of docks being made within a port by a company, the right is granted to them of taking tolls from all vessels coming into the port within which the docks are situated, irrespective of whether the ships come into or use the docks. A naked toll of this description not dependent on the use of the docks themselves, is not to be included among the receipts of the docks.[2] Tenant's Profits are not to be allowed as a deduction where a demise under which a tenant might receive a profit would be illegal under the Dock Company's Act.[3] In the case of docks apportionment has been allowed to be made by acreage on the ground of the impracticability of following the parochial principle strictly.[4] In *R.* v. *Durham (Earl of)*,[5] the apportionment was made in the ratio of the number of ships that entered each parish within the port.

---

[1] 20 L. J. M. C. 155 ; 14 Q. B. 587. See also *Tyne Improvement Commissioners* v. *Cherton*, 1 E. & E. 516 ; s. c. *R.* v. *Cherton*, 32 L. J. M. C. 192 ; s. c. *R.* v. *Tyne Improvement Commissioners*, 6 L. T. N. S. 489.

[2] *R.* v. *Bristol Dock Co.*, 10 L. J. M. C. 105 ; 1 Q. B. 535 ; *R.* v. *Kingston-upon-Hull Dock Co.*, 14 L. J. M. C. 114 ; 7 Q. B. 2. See page 27, supra.

[3] *Mersey Docks & Harbour Board* v. *Liverpool*, L. R. 9 Q. B. 84 ; 43 L. J. M. C. 33.

[4] *R.* v. *Kingston-upon-Hull Dock Co.* (2nd case), 21 L. J. M. C. 153 ; 18 Q. B. 325.

[5] 28 L. J. M. C. 232 ; s. c. *Durham (Earl of)* v. *Bishopwearmouth*, 2 E. & E. 230.

## GAS AND WATER COMPANIES.

Gas[1] and Water Companies may conveniently be con-  *Gas and water*
sidered together, for the nature of their respective properties  *companies,*
is very similar.  They are each occupiers of land, firstly, by  *are occupiers*
what may be called their headquarters, where gas is manu-  *of land by their*
*central works,*
factured or water collected, and, secondly, by the systems of
mains or pipes,[2] by which they deliver the gas or water to their  *and by their*
customers in the various parishes within the area they supply;  *mains.*
and they are of course rateable in each parish on the value
of their occupation there.

Their receipts consist almost entirely of payments made  *Mains rated as*
for gas or water, and the mains by which the gas or water  *direct, and*
*central works*
is delivered (or, more strictly speaking perhaps, the junctions  *as indirect,*
between those mains and the service pipes belonging to their  *sources of*
*profit.*
customers) are the directly productive part of the property,[3]  *see p. 138*
and the central works, &c., are the indirect sources of profit.
The first step is to ascertain the rateable value of the whole
of the mains,[4] by starting with the gross receipts and deducting from them the rateable value of the indirectly productive
parts of the property, (which are to be separately rated in
the parishes where they are situated,)[5] as well as the other
items[6] which, according to the principles explained on pages

---

[1] An example of the rating of a Gas
Company may be found in *R. v. Lee,*
L. R. 1 Q. B. 241 ; 35 L. J. M. C. 105.

[2] *R.* v. *Bath (Corporation of),* 14
East, 609 ; *R.* v. *Rochdale Waterworks,*
1 M. & S. 634 ; *R.* v. *Chelsea Water-
works* (where it is pointed out that it
is immaterial that another person is
rated for the *surface* of the land), 5 B.
& Ad. 156 ; *R.* v. *West Middlesex
Waterworks,* 28 L. J. M. C. 135 ; 1 E.
& E. 716 ; *R.* v. *Brighton Gas Light
Co.,* 5 B. & C. 466 ; 8 Dow. & Ry. 308.

[3] *R.* v. *Mile End Old Town,* 16 L. J.
M. C. 184 ; 10 Q. B. 208.  But see
per Wightman, J., in *R.* v. *West
Middlesex Waterworks,* 28 L. J. M. C.
135, at 140 ; 1 E. & E. 716, at 728.

[4] *R.* v. *Lee,* L. R. 1 Q. B. 241 ;
35 L. J. M. C. 105.

[5] *R.* v. *Mile End Old Town,* 16
L. J. M. C. 184 ; 10 Q. B. 208 ;
*R.* v. *Cambridge Gas Co.,* 7 L. J. M.
C. 50 ; 8 A. & E. 73.

[6] As to what portions of the
ordinary plant and apparatus of a

146 to 151, supra, are proper to be deducted. We then have the rateable value of the whole of the mains, and from that we have to arrive at the rateable value of the mains in each parish by a process of apportionment. It is not correct to make the apportionment according to the quantity of land occupied by the apparatus in each parish,[1] but the share of the total rateable value of the mains is to be in the ratio of the gross receipts in the parish to the total gross receipts. It should perhaps be pointed out that apportionment in the ratio of gross receipts is here no departure from the principle of taking the net profits in the parish as the basis of assessment ; for where the total of expense is taken to be common to the whole apparatus, the ratio of gross receipts is the same as the ratio of net profits,[2] and therefore by using gross receipts as the basis we arrive at the same result as we should by using net profits, and with less calculation. As to waterworks in the hands of commissioners or a corporation restricted by statute from making the same profits as private speculators, see pages 89 and 90, supra.

### TRAMWAY COMPANIES.

Tramway companies occupy land by their rails[3] as gas and water companies do by their pipes. If the entire system be

*Marginal notes:*
Apportionment,

in ratio of gross receipts in the parish.

Restricted occupiers.

Tramway companies, occupiers of

---

Gas Company are to be considered as purchased with Tenant's Capital, and what are to be regarded as belonging to the landlord, see *R.* v. *Lee,* L. R. 1 Q. B. 241 ; 35 L. J. M. C. 105.

[1] *Chelsea Waterworks Co.* v. *Putney,* 22 L. J. M. C. 236 ; s. c. *R.* v. *Putney (Overseers of),* 3 E. & E. 108. It is true that in *R.* v. *Cambridge Gas Co.,* 7 L. J. M. C. 50 ; 8 A. & E. 73, a mileage system of apportionment was applied, but that was on the ground that it was "impossible to suppose any superiority in one

part of the apparatus over another." If that was so in that case, it was one of those cases where the mileage system might be used because it would give the same result as the parochial principle. (See page 117, supra). But see *R.* v. *Sheffield Gas Co.,* 32 L. J. M. C. 169 ; 4 B. & S. 135.

[2] *R.* v. *Mile End Old Town,* 16 L. J. M. C. 184, at 188 ; 10 Q. B. 208, at 220.

[3] *Pimlico Tramways Co.* v. *Greenwich,* L. R. 9 Q. B. 9 ; 43 L. J. M. C. 29.

within one parish, the rateable value is ascertained by land in respect merely making the proper deductions, on the principles of their rails. already explained, from the gross receipts. When, as is more often the case, the system extends into more than one parish, some guidance in fixing the rateable value in each parish containing a portion of the tramway, may be obtained from the case of *The London Tramways Co.* v. *Lambeth.*[1] In that case, Apportionment the respondent parish contained not merely a portion of one —London<br>Tramways Co. route or line of tramway, but portions of five routes, while a v. Lambeth. sixth route was entirely within it. Separate accounts were kept of the earnings on each route, but not of the expenses, except the horse expenses. Under those circumstances it was held that in calculating the net profits of the part of the system within the parish, which according to the parochial principle would be the index of rateable value, the most correct practicable method of apportionment was to allot to the part within the parish of each route, a share of the receipts and horse expenses of that route in the ratio of mileage, and to the part within the parish of the entire system, a share of the total general expenses in the ratio of the number of car-miles run in the parish to the total number run on the system.

——————————————

## BRIDGES.

Approach roads to a bridge come under the head of indi- Bridges—The rect sources of profit.[2] If, as is often the case, a bridge is approaches are<br>indirect sources partly in one parish and partly in another, the rateable value of profit. of the whole must be divided between those parishes in proportion to the length of the bridge in each of them,[3] and it

----

[1] 31 L. T. N. S. 319. (Before the Assistant Judge at Middlesex Sessions.)

[2] *R.* v. *Hammersmith Bridge Co.,* 18 L. J. M. C. 85; 15 Q. B. 369.

[3] Ib.

makes no difference whether tolls are actually taken at both ends of the bridge, or at one end only ;[1] for it is immaterial where profits are received, they are rateable where they are earned; and every portion of the span of the bridge contributes equally to earn the tolls, therefore the mileage system of apportionment may be employed. See also *R.* v. *Blackfriars Bridge Co.*[2]

## MINES.

**Mines.**

Mines fall under three heads, 1st, where the royalty or dues are for the time being wholly reserved in kind ; 2nd, tin lead, or copper mines not coming under the 1st head ; and 3rd, mines not falling under either of the above heads.

**1st. Where royalty reserved in kind.**

**Old law.**

**Reservation of ore.**

**Of metal.**

**Of dressed ore.**

**1st. Where the royalty or dues are for the time being wholly reserved in kind.**—While the exemption from rating of mines other than coal mines existed, it was nevertheless held that if a landlord reserved to himself a proportion of the ore, he was thereby constituted an occupier of land, or rather that in respect of the reserved ore he remained in occupation, and was rateable as an occupier.[3] It was not so however if the reservation was of a portion of the metal obtained from the ore by smelting, for that is a manufactured article rather than a part of the original earth itself,[4] but ore in a dressed state fit for smelting was within the rule,[5] and so was a reser-

---

[1] *R.* v. *Barnes,* 1 B. & Ad. 113.

[2] 8 L. T. M. C. 29 ; 9 A. & E. 828.

[3] *R.* v. *St. Austell,* 5 B. & Ad. 623 ; 1 Dow. & Ry. 351 ; *R.* v. *Baptist Mill Co.,* 1 M. & S. 612 ; *R.* v. *St. Agnes,* 3 T. R. 480; *Rowls*

v. *Gells,* Cowp. 451 ; *Crease* v. *Sawle,* 11 L. J. M. C. 62 ; 2 Q. B. 862 ; *R.* v. *Todd,* 10 L. J. M. C. 14; 12 A. & E. 816.

[4] *R.* v. *Pomfret,* 5 M. & S. 139.

[5] *R.* v. *St. Austell,* 5 B. & Ad. 693 ; 1 Dow. & Ry. 351.

vation of a royalty in kind with an option to receive it in money.[1] Before the Rating Act of 1874 the above was settled law in regard to mines that were not then rateable in themselves, and that Act, while making all mines rateable, preserved the above rules as they previously existed.[2] . When a mine is let on those terms, the lessor is rateable on the royalties and the tenant on the machinery and plant.[3] Royalty in kind with option to receive it in money.<br>The above not altered by the Rating Act, 1874.

**2nd.  Tin, lead, or copper mines, except where the royalty or dues are for the time being wholly reserved in kind.—** The 7th section of the Rating Act, 1874, is as follows: "Where a tin, lead, or copper mine is occupied under a lease or leases granted without fine on a reservation wholly or partly of dues or rent, the gross value [4] of the mine shall be taken to be the annual amount of the whole of the dues payable in respect thereof during the year ending on the 31st day of December preceding the date at which the valuation list is made, in addition to the annual amount of any fixed rent reserved for the same which may not be paid or satisfied by such dues. 2nd. Tin, lead, or copper mines not falling under 1st head.<br><br>Gross value.

"The rateable annual value of such mine shall be the same as the gross value thereof, except that where the person receiving the dues or rent is liable for repairs, insurance, or other expenses necessary to maintain the mine in a state to command the annual amount of dues or rent, the average annual cost of the repairs, insurance, and other expenses for which he is so liable, shall be deducted from the gross value for the purpose of calculating the rateable value. Rateable value.

---

[1] *Van Mining Co.* v. *Llanidloes,* 1 Ex. D. 310 ; 45 L. J. M. C. 138.

[2] 37 & 38 Vict. c. 54, sec. 13.

[3] *Van Mining Co.* v. *Llanidloes,* 1 Ex. D. 310; 45 L. J. M. C. 138 ; *Talargoch Mining Co.* v. *St. Asaph Union,* L. R. 3 Q. B. 478; 37 L. J. M. C. 149 ; *Guest* v. *East Dean,* L. R. 7 Q. B. 334 ; 41 L. J. M. C. 129 ;

*Kitlow* v. *Liskeard Union,* L. R. 10 Q. B. 7 ; 44 L. J. M. C. 23.

[4] In this Act, unless the context otherwise requires, the term "Gross Value" has the same meaning as "Gross Estimated Rental" in the Union Assessment Committee Act, 1862. See sec. 15.

In certain cases
gross and rate-
able value is
the
" In the following cases, namely :—

> " (1) Where any such mine is occupied under a lease
> granted wholly or partly on a fine ; and
>
> " (2) Where any such mine is occupied and worked by
> the owner ; and
>
> " (3) In the case of any other such mine which is not
> excepted from the provisions of this Act, and to
> which the foregoing provisions of this section do
> not apply ;

the gross and rateable annual value of the mine shall be
taken to be the annual amount of the dues or dues and rent

rent on lease,
not on yearly
tenancy.
at which the mine might be reasonably expected to let without fine *on a lease of the ordinary duration according to
the usage of the country,*[1] if the tenant undertook to pay all
tenant's rates and taxes, and tithe rent-charge, and also the
repairs, insurance, and other expenses necessary to maintain
the mine in a state to command such annual amount of dues,

Who may be
rated.
or dues and rent.

" The purser, secretary, and chief managing agent for the
time being, of any tin, lead, or copper mine, or any of them,
may, if the overseers or other rating authority think fit, be
rated as the occupier thereof.

Definitions.
Mine.
" In this section,—

> " The term ' mine,' when a mine is occupied under a lease,
> includes the underground workings and the engines,
> machinery, workshops, tramways, and other plant,
> buildings (not being dwelling-houses), and works and
> surface of land occupied in connexion with and for the
> purposes of the mine, and situate within the bounda-
> ries of the land comprised in the lease or leases under
> which the dues, or dues and rent, are payable or
> reserved :

Dues.
> " The term ' dues ' means dues, royalty or toll, either in

---

[1] N. B.—Not on a yearly tenancy as in the case of other hereditaments.

money, or partly in money and partly in kind, and the amount of dues which are reserved in kind means the value of such dues:

"The term 'lease' means lease or sett, or licence to work, or agreement for a lease or sett, or licence to work:     *Lease.*

"The term 'fine' means fine, premium or profit, or other payment or consideration in the nature thereof."     *Fine.*

The 8th and 9th sections provide for the deduction of rates[1] by the tenants of mines that were not rateable previous to the Act.   •

3rd. **All mines not falling under either the 1st or 2nd heads.** —This class comprises (*a*) coal mines,[2] and (*b*) mines, other than tin, lead, or copper, ~~first made rateable by the Act of 1874~~,[3] provided of course that the royalty or dues <u>are not</u> wholly reserved in kind.     3rd. All mines not falling under the 1st or 2nd heads.

The basis of assessment for this class will be the rent of the hypothetical tenant of the Parochial Assessment <u>Act.</u> This must be ascertained in accordance with the general principles already laid down in the case of other hereditaments. It may be mentioned that among the deductions, the margin to be allowed for tenant's profit will probably be a     Rateable under the P. A. Act.

---

[1] *Chaloner* v. *Bolckow*, 3 App. Cas. 933 ; 47 L. J. C. P. 562 ; *Devonshire (Duke)* v. *Barrow Hæmatite Co.*, 2 Q. B. D. 286 ; 46 L. J. Q. B. 435.

[2] *R.* v. *Attwood*, 6 B. & C. 277, and *R.* v. *Granville (Lord)*, 9 B. & C. 188, are cases on the rating of coal mines.

[3] Without expressing an opinion as to the correctness of the suggestion, it may be mentioned that it is suggested in Bainbridge on Mines (4th ed. at page 774), that the word "such" in sec. 7, sub-sec. 3, of the Rating Act, 1874 (see on page 160,

supra) should probably be omitted. If it were omitted the mines in group (*b*) above would have been rateable under that sub section, and would have fallen within the 2nd class ; but as the sub-section stands, they are clearly not within it, and the Act merely makes them rateable without directing how they are to be rated. They must therefore be assessed in accordance with the Parochial Assessment Act, namely, on the basis of the rent of a yearly tenant, instead of the rent of a tenant holding under a lease. As to royalties see pp. 96-98 supra.

liberal one, on account of the risk and uncertainty of mining operations.

**Where mine not wholly within one parish.** Where a mine is not wholly within the parish where the shaft or pit is situated, it is not to be rated as a whole in that parish, but each parish into which it extends must rate the part within it.[1] There do not, however, appear to be any reported decisions as to the method in which the rateable value of the mine in a parish which contains only some of the underground workings, is to be estimated.

As to the rating of quarries see pages 96 to 98 supra.[2]

## TITHES.

**Tithes are within the P. A. Act.** Tithes are hereditaments within the Parochial Assessment Act,[3] and therefore are to be assessed in accordance with the standard of rateable value therein prescribed. But of the **But the deductions there specified are not applicable to tithes,** allowances and deductions specified in the Parochial Assessment Act some, for instance, ' tithe commutation rent-charge ' and ' insurance ' are inapplicable to tithes, while on the other hand, the tithe owner, as such, is commonly subject to charges and outgoings, such as tenths and other ecclesiastical dues, which are not specified in the Act, but which it is necessary to deduct in order to arrive at the prescribed basis of rateable value, namely, <u>the rent reasonably to be expected</u>. This must be in all cases ascertained if rating is to be uniform ; and such deductions fall within the principle of the Act, for its main object was to effect uniformity of rating. In order then to give proper effect to the Act, the deductions **therefore they are to be** and allowances specified in it, must be considered as instances

[1] *R.* v. *Foleshill*, 4 L. J. M. C. 63;      *Attwood*, 6 B. & C. 277.
2 A. & E. 593.      [3] *R.* v. *Capel*, 9 L. J. M. C. 65 ;
[2] See also per Abbott J. in *R.* v.      12 A. & E. 382.

applicable to one great class of property, and not as a com- regarded as<br>examples,
plete enumeration of all those that are applicable to every class;
and in the assessment of tithes, which belong to a different
class, analogy is the guide to the admissibility of deductions.
That analogy should be " as large and liberal as is necessary and such de-<br>ductions made
to effectuate substantial equality in the assessment, and at as are analo-
the same time compatible with the maintenance of the gous in<br>principle to
principle." [1] them.

The following list of deductions, allowable or the contrary, Deductions in<br>the case of
is not intended as an exhaustive one; it only comprises those tithes.
which have been the subject of judicial decision, and the admissibility of any others which may be suggested must be
determined by general principles and the analogy of the
deductions that are allowed in the case of corporeal hereditaments:—

(1) Expenses of collection; [2] Expenses.
Cost of legal proceedings to enforce payment; [3]
Losses by ultimate non-payment; [4]

    *but not* the salary of a curate, or a contribution to the
    stipend of the minister of a district church; [5]

---

[1] Hackney & Lamberhurst Tithe Commutation Rent-charge cases—*R.* v. *Goodchild*, 27 L. J. M. C. 233 ; s. c. *Goodchild* v. *St. John's, Hackney,* E. B. & E. 1.

[2] Ibid.

[3] Ibid.

[4] Ibid.

[5] *R.* v: *Jodrell,* 1 B. & Ad. 403 ; *R.* v. *Sherford,* L. R. 2 Q. B. 503 ; 36 L. J. M. C. 113. In *R.* v. *Goodchild* it was held that these were allowable deductions if the vicar was under a legal obligation to pay them, or if he was under a moral obligation to provide himself with assistance in addition to (not in substitution for) his own services, in order properly to supply the wants of the parish. *R.* v. *Goodchild,* was a binding authority upon this point till the *Mersey Dock Cases,* 35 L. J. M. C. 1 ; 11 H. L. C. 443. See *Williams* v. *Llangeinwen,* 31 L. J. M. C. 54 ; 1 B. & S. 699 ; *Wheeler* v. *Burmington,* 31 L. J. M. C. 57 ; 1 B. & S. 709, and *Scriven-with-Tentergate* v. *Fawcett,* 32 L. J. M. C. 161 ; 3 B. & S. 797. But as was pointed out in *R.* v. *Sherford,* the *Mersey Dock Cases* impliedly overruled *R.* v. *Goodchild* upon this point by laying down the rule that where property yields a profit the occupier is rateable upon that profit no matter where it goes to.

or any sum in respect of personal services as officiating minister; [1]

or payments to the Governors of Queen Anne's Bounty in liquidation of the principal and interest of a loan on mortgage of the tithes.[2]

**Rates and taxes.**

(2) Poor rate and other usual tenant's rates and taxes incident to the occupation, e.g. General Rate and Lighting Rate and Tenant's Property Tax; [3]

First Fruits, Tenths and any other ecclesiastical dues of a similar nature; [4]

but not Land Tax, for it does not usually fall on the tenant.[5]

**Tenant's profits —allowance small if any.**

(3) Tenant's Profits.—No one would become a tenant without the inducement of some profit,[6] but the margin of profit necessary to tempt a tenant to take, who was to be guaranteed by the above mentioned allowance against the expense of collection, bad debts, and law expenses, would probably be but small in the case of tithes, where the receipts may be estimated with considerable certainty, compared, for instance, with what would be required where there is more risk and uncertainty, as in the case of a mine. In *R.* v. *Goodchild*,[7] no further allowance was made for Tenant's Profits, but that was apparently on the assumption that the tenant would pocket something on the allowance there made for collection.

**Repairs of the chancel—**

In a circular of the Poor Law Board, dated May 9th, 1859,

---

[1] *R.* v. *Joddrell*, 1 B. & Ad. 403 ; Hackney & Lamberhurst Tithe Commutation Rent-charge cases—*R.* v. *Goodchild*, 27 L. J. M. C. 233, s. c. *Goodchild* v. *St. John's, Hackney*, E. B. & E. 1.

[2] Hackney & Lamberhurst Tithe Commutation Rent-charge Cases—*R.* v. *Hawkins*, 27 L. J. M. C. 248 ; s. c.

*Hawkins* v. *Lamberhurst*, E. B. & E. 55.

[3] *R.* v. *Goodchild*, supra note [1].

[4] Ibid.

[5] Ibid.

[6] Ibid. and *R.* v. *Capel*, 9 L. J. M. C. 65 ; 12 A. & E. 382.

[7] Supra note [1].

(before the *Mersey Dock Cases*), it is directed that an allow- probably not allowable as a deduction.
ance is to be made for repairs to the chancel, but there do not
appear to be any judicial decisions on the point, and it is
apprehended that such a deduction would not be admissible
since the *Mersey Dock Cases.*

Where tithes have been commuted under the General Payments in commutation under the Act of 1836 rateable,
Tithe Commutation Act of 1836, the tithe commutation rent-
charge is rateable in like manner as the tithe for which it is
substituted;[1] and where tithes have been commuted by
local or private acts, in the city of London or elsewhere, the under local or private Act, depends on the terms of the Act,
rateability of the payments in commutation depends on the
terms of the particular Act. Unless the Act in question provides that the payments are to be free from poor rates they
are rateable on the general principle which was established
before the General Commutation Act, that any composition,
modus, or assessment in lieu of tithe is rateable in like
manner as the tithe itself.[2]

Where it is provided that such payments are to be free if free of rate not to be deducted by the occupier.
from poor rate, and therefore the vicar is not rateable,[3] then
they are not allowed as a deduction in estimating the rateable value of the occupation of the occupier who pays them.[4]

---

## SALEABLE UNDERWOODS, PLANTATIONS, AND WOODS.

The Rating Act of 1874,[5] enacts by section 4, that "The Rating Act of 1874. Section 4.
gross and rateable value of any land used for a plantation or

---

[1] 6 & 7 Will. IV. c. 71, sec. 69.
[2] *Lowndes* v. *Horne,* 2 Wm. Bl.
1252; *R.* v. *Toms,* 1 Dougl. 401; *Rann*
v. *Pickin,* Cald. 196; *R.* v. *Boldero,*
4 B. & C. 467; 6 Dow. & Ry. 557.
[3] *Chatfield* v. *Rushton,* 3 B. & C.

863; *Mitchell* v. *Fordham,* 5 L. J. (O.
S.) M. C. 79; 6 B. & C. 274; *R.* v.
*Shaw,* 17 L. J. M. C. 137; 12 Q. B. 419.
[4] *Hackett* v. *Long Bennington,* 33
L. J. M. C. 137; 16 C. B. N. S. 38.
[5] 37 & 38 Vict. c. 54.

a wood, or for the growth of saleable underwood, shall be estimated as follows :—

Sub-sec. (a).

"(a) If the land is used <u>only for a plantation or a wood,</u> the value shall be estimated as if the land, instead of being a plantation or a wood, were let and occupied in its <u>natural and</u> unimproved state."

It has been decided that the value of sporting rights is to be taken into account in estimating, under sec. 4, sub-sec. (a), the rateable value of the land in its natural and unimproved state.[1]

Sub-sec. (b).

"(b) If the land is used for the <u>growth of saleable under-wood,</u> the value shall be estimated as if the land were let for that purpose."

In rating land under sub-sec. (b), if it is not actually let, the data for estimating the rent it might reasonably be expected to fetch, will be the profits it produces <u>communibus annis.</u> Underwoods actually produce profit, not every year but only once in so many years, when they are cut down. The annual profit must therefore be calculated by dividing the profit produced in the year in which they are cut down, by the number of years during which they are allowed to grow before being cut.[2]

Sub.-sec. (c).

"(c) If the land is used <u>both for a plantation or a wood and the growth of saleable underwood,</u> the value shall be estimated either as if the land were used only for a plantation or a wood, <u>or</u> as if the land were used only for the growth of the saleable underwood growing thereon, <u>as the assessment committee may determine.</u>"

Section 5.

Section 5 provides that any tenant holding under a lease or agreement made previous to the Act, such land as is referred to in section 4, sub-secs. (a) and (c), may deduct from

---

[1] *Eyton* v. *Mold*, 6 Q. B. D. 13 ; 50 L. J. M. C. 39.

[2] See *R.* v. *Mirfield*, 10 East, 219, and page 94, *supra*.

his rent, during the continuance of the lease or agreement the rates due to any increase in his rateable value caused by the Act.

---

## RIGHTS OF SHOOTING, FISHING, ETC.

The Rating Act of 1874[1] provides by section 6 as follows :— Sporting rights.
" (1) Where any right of fowling, or of shooting, or of Rating Act 1874. taking or killing game or rabbits, or of fishing (hereinafter Section 6. referred to as a right of sporting), is severed from the occu- Sub-sec. (1). pation of the land and is not let, and the owner of such right receives rent for the land, the said right shall not be separately valued or rated, but the gross and rateable value of the land shall be estimated as if the said right were not severed ; and in such case if the rateable value is increased by reason of its being so estimated, but not otherwise, the occupier of the land may (unless he has specifically contracted to pay such rate in the event of an increase) deduct from his rent such portion of any poor or other local rate as is paid by him in respect of such increase ; and every assessment committee, on the application of the occupier, shall certify in the valuation list or otherwise the fact and amount of such increase.

" (2) Where any right of sporting, when severed[2] from the Sub-sec. (2). occupation of the land, is let, either the owner or the lessee thereof, according as the persons making the rate determine, may be rated as the occupier thereof.

" (3) Subject to the foregoing provisions of this section the Sub-sec. (3).

---

[1] 37 & 38 Vict. c. 54.
[2] See *Kenrick* v. *Guilsfield*, 5 C. P. D. 41 ; 49 L. J. M. C. 27.

owner of any right of sporting, when severed from the occupation of the land, may be rated as the occupier thereof.

Sub-sec. (4). "(4) For the purposes of this section, the person, who, if the right of sporting is not let, is entitled to exercise the right, or who, if the right is let, is entitled to receive the rent for the same, shall be deemed to be the owner of the right."

When not severed from the occupation indirectly rateable. The above provisions relate to the rating of sporting rights, only when severed from the occupation of the land. When not severed they are, as they were before this Act, indirectly rated, by assessing the land at the amount for which it would let to a yearly tenant, its value being enhanced by its capacity for sporting purposes.[1]

## LUNATIC ASYLUMS.

Lunatic asylums. There is a statutory provision with regard to the rating of Lunatic Asylums, which, as it relates rather to quantum than to rateability in the abstract, may be more appropriately placed in this division of the work than in that where the total exemptions from rateability by statute are placed.

It was provided by the 16 & 17 Vict. c. 97, sec. 35, that "no lands or buildings already or to be hereafter purchased or acquired, under the provisions of any former Act or this Act, for the purpose of any asylum (with or without any additional building erected or to be erected thereon), shall while used for such purposes be assessed to any county, Rateability limited to parochial, or other local rates *at a higher value or more*

---

[1] *Fyton* v. *Mold*, 6 Q. B. D. 13; 50 L. J. M. C. 39. See also *Hilton & Walkerfield* v. *Bowes*, L. R. 1 Q. B. 359; 35 L. J. M. C. 137;    *R.* v. *Battle*, L. R. 2 Q. B. 8; 36 L. J. M. C. 1; *R.* v. *Williams*, 2 L. T. O. S. 76.

*improved rent than the value or rent at which the same* value of land
*were assessed at the time of such purchase or acquisition."* or buildings
when pur-
Used 'for the purposes of any asylum,' was held in *Congreve* chased.
v. *Upton,*[1] to cover the residence appropriated to a medical Residence of doctor,
superintendent although not within the asylum walls, but
not a residence without the walls appropriated to the and chaplain.
chaplain; the distinction apparently being based on the fact
that the former is, but the latter is not, required by the Act
to be resident.

It was held in *R.* v. *Fulbourn,*[2] that a farm and garden Farm and
partly cultivated by the lunatics were 'used for the purposes garden.
of the asylum' and entitled to the benefit of the section,
although profit was made from them, provided that their
primary object was, not profit, but the healthful employment
of the lunatics.

---

## LAND GENERALLY—METROPOLIS VALUATION ACT.

All rateable hereditaments falling under the general head Other here-
of 'lands,' which have not been made the subject of special ditaments
rateable on
mention, are to be rated in accordance with the Parochial general
principles.
Assessment Act and the general principles which have been
elucidated above. (Pages 81 to 141.)

It should be remembered that 'land' includes not only 'Land' not
the face of the earth but everything under or over it.[3] limited to the
surface of the
"Land hath in its legal significations an indefinite extent, earth.
upwards as well as downwards."[4] The parish authorities

---

[1] 33 L. J. M. C. 83; 4 B. & S.          [3] *Electric Telegraph Co.* v. *Salford,*
857.                                      24 L. J. M. C. 146; 11 Ex. 181.
[2] 34 L. J. M. C. 106; 6 B. & S.         [4] Burn's Justice, Vol. IV., p. 190
451.                                      (29th edition).

are therefore entitled to as many separate contributions to the poor rate as there are in existence separate rateable occupations, whether on, above, or below the surface. For instance, there may be separate rateable occupations one above the other, in respect of a mine, gas and water mains, a tramway, a bridge, and a telegraph wire.

Rating in the metropolis,

*Metropolis Valuation Act.*—The rating of property within the metropolis is governed by the Valuation (Metropolis) Act of 1869.[1] That Act, however, did not interfere with the general principles of rating. Its object was to promote uniformity, and it mainly deals with matters of procedure. It contains a better definition of 'gross estimated rental' (for which it substitutes the term 'gross value') than previously existed ; namely, "The term 'gross value,' means the annual rent which a tenant might reasonably be expected, taking one year with another, to pay for an hereditament, if the tenant undertook to pay all usual tenant's rates and taxes, and tithe commutation rent-charge, if any, and if the landlord undertook to bear the cost of the repairs and insurance, and the other expenses, if any, necessary to maintain the hereditament in a state to command that rent. The term ' rateable value,' means the gross value after deducting therefrom the probable average cost of the repairs, insurance, and other expenses as aforesaid."

Metropolis Valuation Act. Definitions of gross and rateable value.

Limit of deductions.

It also divided rateable hereditaments into eleven classes, and fixed a proportion or percentage for each respective class, as the maximum allowable by way of deduction from the gross value in calculating the rateable value. For instance, in class 1, consisting of houses and buildings, or either of them, without land other than gardens, where the gross value is under £20, the maximum of such deductions is fixed at 25 per cent., or one-fourth ; and in class 8, consisting of mills

----

[1] 32 & 33 Vict. c. 67.

and manufactories, the maximum deduction is 33⅓ per cent., or one-third; but no maximum is fixed for the classes which contain tithes, railways, waterworks, &c.; in respect of which the deductions are to be determined according to the circumstances and the general principles of law.

*1ˢᵗ Reading - Aug. 10ᵗʰ 1896.*

.

# INDEX.

CONTROL BY LANDLORD,
>inconsistent with rateability of tenant, 47—57
>so is even a power of control, although not exercised, 49, 50

COPROLITES, 67

CORPORATION,
>occupying waterworks under restrictions as to profits, 89, 90
>occupiers of common subject to right of pasturage in freemen, 73

CORPUS EXHAUSTED BY OCCUPIER,
>as in the cases of brickfields, cemeteries, and quarries, 99, 100

COUNTY JUSTICES,
>when rateable for Assize Courts, &c., 80

CROWN,
>property occupied by the, not rateable, 34, 74—80
>or by servants of the Crown as its agents, 74
>but subjects occupying Crown property for their own benefit are rateable, 79
>and so are servants of the Crown if their occupation is in excess of what is necessary for their service, 79

CURATE,
>salary of not a deduction in rating tithes, 163

DEDUCTIONS ALLOWABLE,
>from rent—repairs, insurance, &c., 84
>from gross receipts—working expenses, value of indirect sources of profit, tenant's deductions, and landlord's deductions, 144—150

DEDUCTIONS NOT ALLOWABLE, 151

DEFENCE OF THE REALM,
>lands taken under statute for, rateable at then existing value only, 75

DEFICIENCY,
>in rates during construction of Railway, 151

DEMISE,
>whether demise or license depends on substance of the agreement rather than the particular words used, 45

DIFFERENT OCCUPIERS,
>of parts of a house separately rateable, 62

DIRECT AND INDIRECT SOURCES OF PROFIT,
>distinction between, 138
>how each to be rated, 140

DISCRETIONARY EXEMPTION,
>of Sunday and Ragged Schools, 26

THE END.

BRADBURY, AGNEW, & CO., PRINTERS, WHITEFRIARS.

www.ingramcontent.com/pod-product-compliance
Lightning Source LLC
Chambersburg PA
CBHW030831270326
41928CB00007B/993